Hallandale Beach Florida

It might look like…nothing, but this incredible view, taken by an unknown photographer sometime in November 1924, shows today's Hallandale Beach, just west of the Hallandale Beach Boulevard location of the Florida East Coast Railway depot. "Incredible!" is simply an understatement.

Hallandale Beach Florida

For More than Ninety Years Broward County's City of Choice

Seth H. Bramson

THE History PRESS

Published by The History Press
Charleston, SC 29403
www.historypress.net

First published 2010

Manufactured in the United States

ISBN 978.1.59629.961.0

Bramson, Seth, 1944-
Hallandale Beach, Florida : for more than ninety years Broward County's city of choice /
Seth H. Bramson.
p. cm.
ISBN 978-1-59629-961-0
1. Hallandale (Fla.)--History. 2. Hallandale (Fla.)--Social life and customs. 3. Hallandale (Fla.)--Economic conditions. 4. Hallandale (Fla.)--Biography. I. Title.
F319.H35B73 2010
975.9'35--dc22
2010018194

This book is dedicated to two groups of Hallandale and Hallandale Beach pioneers. In the first group are the original founders of what would some day become, in a future that they would not live to see, a great city. Among those who must be properly recognized posthumously for all that they did so long ago are James E. Ingraham, Luther Halland, Olof Zetterlund, Rosina and Frank Curci and August and Henry L. Gieges.

The second group are the four modern-day Hallandale Beach pioneers who worked arduously and endlessly to ensure that the history of this incredible city would be properly commemorated through the publication of this book. Without their efforts to preserve Hallandale Beach's history and to memorialize it for posterity, this book might not have been written.

And so it is, therefore, to the happily very much alive Jim Curci, John Hardwick, Vice-mayor Bill Julian and Eddie Pickett, who have each spent a lifetime in Hallandale and Hallandale Beach and whose lives represent the hopes, dreams and ideals of the founders who were their predecessors, that this book is warmly and gratefully dedicated.

Contents

Mayor Joy Cooper

CITY OF HALLANDALE BEACH
City of Choice

400 South Federal Highway ~ Hallandale Beach, Florida 33009
954.457.1318 ~ fax 954.457.1454 ~ joycooper@aol.com
www.mayorjoycooper.com

Greetings,

It is an honor to be serving as mayor during such an exciting time in Hallandale Beach. Being the first directly elected mayor in Hallandale Beach I am extremely proud to be part of a visionary commission that has set in motion a plan to reinvent a city rich in history.

My history and love of Florida started over twenty five years ago. In 1985 my husband and I visited South Florida from Philadelphia and we decided to become snowbirds. In 1991 we found a home in Golden Isles and moved to Hallandale Beach full time. We found that Hallandale Beach was a great location and offered all the amenities of a big city. We made it our *City of Choice*. We were also drawn to the unique home town feel of this community. I like to say even though we are a relatively small geographic city of only 4 square miles we are a city with a big heart. We have it all!

Our city has been going through a renaissance over the past 8 years. The progress and commitment to the sustainability of our future has put Hallandale Beach back on the map. We have become a global destination. While our sites our set on the future we must never forget our past.

Being born in Trenton New Jersey and growing up in Levittown Pennsylvania I had the opportunity of having history at my door step. Growing up within the Cradle of Liberty, I have developed a keen interest in history and an understanding of how important it is to preserve a city's heritage. Being part of the commission that has established the first Historical Village in our community, preserved one, if not the oldest school houses in Broward County and now publishing the second book on the history of this great city is a humbling honor.

Documenting the reawaking of Hallandale Beaches racetracks, the reopening of casinos, the development of the city's first town center, the uncovering and preservation of historical facts is so important to the fabric of our community. This book will bring you our rich history and most importantly preserve it for all our residents, visitors and generations to come.

Enjoy!

Joy F Cooper

Mayor Joy Cooper

City of Hallandale Beach

CITY OF HALLANDALE BEACH
City of Choice

Joy F. Cooper, Mayor
William Julian, Vice-Mayor
Keith London, Commissioner
Dorothy Ross, Commissioner
Anthony Sanders, Commissioner

400 South Federal Highway
Hallandale Beach, FL 33009-6433
Phone: (954) 458-3251
Fax: (954) 457-1342
Commission Fax: (954) 457-1454

To the residents of Hallandale Beach,

It is with great pleasure and pride that we present the new and updated history book of our fine City. After many years of research, gathering thousands of pictures and documents, we have produced one of the most complete historical books of any City in Broward County. I must thank our City Manager, Mike Good, his staff of professionals, and our City Commission who have made my many years in the making endeavor possible to complete.

As a lifetime resident and historian of Hallandale Beach, I am proud that this book will be part of my legacy of our City's history. Florida historian, Seth H. Bramson, has done a superb job in the creation of this book. Because of his expertise in historical research and the fact that he is the senior collector of memorabilia in the country, Mr. Bramson has crafted a vibrant tribute to our City.

But the fact is that, without your assistance in the donation and scanning of your family photos and our City's historic memorabilia, records and landmarks, this book would not be complete, and I cannot thank you enough for all that you have done to help us bring this project to a successful conclusion.

As a member of the Broward County Historical Commission, and advisor to our Hallandale Beach Historical Advisory Board, I am pleased to give credit to our Hallandale Historical Board and its President, Ed Pickett, for their invaluable assistance, helping to insure the accuracy and validity of our book.

Again, to the residents of our "City of Choice," thank you,

William "Bill" Julian
Vice-Mayor

City of Hallandale Beach

CITY OF HALLANDALE BEACH
City of Choice

D. Mike Good
City Manager

400 South Federal Highway
Hallandale Beach, FL 33009-6433
Phone: (954) 458-3251
Fax: (954) 457-1342

City Mgr. Fax: (954) 457-1454

Dear friends:

It is a pleasure for me to welcome you to the new history of our city and I am honored to have played a part in making this book possible.

As some of you know, Hallandale Beach was brought to life by the man for whom the city is named, Luther Halland, and his faith in the area, and his work in forming a community which would become the genesis for a town and then a city have now been properly memorialized.

As you will learn in this book, our history goes back to 1897 and the fascinating twists and turns, including Hallandale's being part of the formation of a new county in 1915, surviving several brutal hurricanes, the great boom and bust of the 1920s, becoming a town in 1927 and then a city in 1947, the abolition and re-legalization of casino gaming, the dog and horse tracks and the building of the modern day condominiums, hotels and motels are all a part of our incredible story, of which all of our citizens have been very much a part.

It was a pleasure to work with noted South Florida author Seth H. Bramson and to watch the book progress from genesis to publication and I know that you will greatly enjoy learning about our history as well as the people of all races, creeds and national origins who, as our story unfolded, worked together to help build what is now one of the finest places in America in which to live, work, raise a family or enjoy a vacation, Broward County's City of Choice for more than 90 years, Hallandale Beach, Florida.

Sincerely yours,

D. Mike Good,
City Manager

Acknowledgements

The complete outpouring of interest and willingness to provide material for this book was nothing short of astounding. From the assistance of Mayor Joy Cooper, Vice-mayor William A. (Bill) Julian, commission members Dorothy Ross, Keith S. London and Anthony Sanders, City Manager Mike Good, Assistant City Manager Mark Antonio, Chief of Police Thomas A. Magill, Major Kenneth Cowley, Fire Chief Daniel P. Sullivan and Deputy Chief Art Bousquet to that of Jim Curci, Eddie Pickett (chair of the Historic Preservation Board) and John Hardwick, the cooperation was similar to a fountain of goodwill and good wishes, with memories, material, photographs, information and assistance coming via mail, e-mail, telephone and cellphone in an unending stream.

In a project such as this, an author must make every effort to include each and every person who could be of assistance; hence, if any individual or firm is not included, heartfelt apologies are extended, and I want to thank, with great warmth and sincere gratitude, in addition to those named above, the following: Patricia Genetti, executive director of the Hallandale Beach Chamber of Commerce, for providing innumerable photos of chamber members and activities; Joe Kessel, also of the chamber; Zach Fuerst of Sage Bagel and Deli; Ellen Zimmerman; Pat Saba; John Patchen; David of Tel-Aviv Texaco; Bill Kelley of Bill Bill Kelley Kelley Chevrolet fame; Susan Mandel of Hallandale Creative Printing; famed South Florida photographer Joel Black; Rita Warren, who happily shared her memories of the land crabs on Beach Boulevard and the drive-in theatre on East Hallandale Beach Boulevard where Publix is now located; and Harriet and Bart Bruni of Bestec Exterminators.

A "tip of the Hatlo hat!" must be included to Bill McGoun, who wrote the original history of the city, titled *Hallandale*, which was published in 1976, and to Peter Bluesten, longtime editor and publisher of *Hallandale Digest*, which, for many years, was the city's "hometown newspaper" and which has been an absolute fountain of Hallandale facts, information and history. No work on the history of Hallandale could be considered legitimate if it did not have the book and the newspaper to use as sources.

Larry Blustein, editor, and David Udoff, staff writer of the *South Florida Sun-Times*, gave us unending cooperation and support, and their wonderful articles on and about the book prompted numerous phone calls and personal contacts with Hallandale Beach-ers who provided items for inclusion.

Dan Adkins, vice-president, Vanessa Lopez, public relations coordinator, and Aldo Leone, racing manager of Mardi Gras Casino and Racing (the former Hollywood Dog Track), gave me image after image to use, along with a complete history of and about the track. At Gulfstream Park and Casino, Mike Cronin, assistant to the president for marketing, Caton Bredar, executive producer, media development, and Randy Abraham, media and marketing assistant, "loaded me up" with great "stuff" as well as a complete history of that famous facility.

Joseph R. Lello, chief of the Broward Sheriff's Office Department of Fire Rescue, provided important factual information on the founding of Hallandale's Volunteer Fire Department and its transition to a paid force, while Kathleen Bisson Cianfrani generously shared Hallandale photos and information on the city as well as on her dad, Francis C. "Biz" Bisson, who served as the city's first paid fire chief; we are very grateful to both Kathleen and Chief Lello for their assistance. Hallandale Beach Police CSI Chris Redfern provided an excellent disc of police department images, and we thank Chris for his careful and caring work.

The ladies in the Hallandale Beach city manager's office were wonderful and always anxious to be of assistance, and I extend warm thanks for their help to Jennifer M. Frastai, city manager administrator; Shari Canada, deputy city clerk; and Minerva Ozuna, administrative office assistant.

Our friends at the Hallandale Beach Rotary Club, including but not limited to Helmut Meissner and Robert Friedman, turned over the complete history of the club for our use, while the entire membership of that fine organization was totally supportive. Keith Schuit, manager of the Hallandale

Beach branch of the Community Bank of Broward County, "couldn't do enough" and provided material on the history of the Donn family, who owned Gulfstream for many years, while Doug Donn was never too busy to speak with me and was a fountain of information regarding his illustrious family and the track.

My friend of more than XX years, Bernard ("Buddy") Gertner, introduced me to Gale Barnett Kappes, and she, her husband Harry and brother Billy provided history and photographs of the original Barnett's, its first truck and its people. Bernie Harrold, general manager of Holiday Bowling Center, gave us wonderful photos and information of and from that business.

"Toula" of Flashback Diner, Iris Fuerst and son Zachary of Sage Bagel and Deli and Jacqueline Ortiz and Ignacio Dominguez of Nick's Restaurant were very helpful in providing pictures of their respective establishments.

From the Palms community, special thanks are extended to Willie Washington, Mary Washington, Virginia Kilpatrick, Craig Anderson, Qunea Gordon, Eva Williams and Derrick Wallace for their loans of photographs and memorabilia.

To Denyse Cunningham, curator of the Broward County Historical Commission and Museum in Fort Lauderdale, who not only gave generously of her time but also provided us with numerous superb Hallandale Beach images, a special note of thanks.

As with several previous books, Adam Rogers, the young man who is our webmaster and IT director, went "above and beyond the call of duty" to make certain that all of the pictures were usable and all of the copy was to our publisher's specs, and we are most grateful to him for his caring and quality work.

Unless otherwise credited, all photographs are from the collection of the author.
Photographs from the files of the City of Hallandale Beach are shown with the credit *CoHB*.
Photographs from the files of the Broward County Historical Commission and Museum are shown with the credit *BCHC*.

Introduction

In order to understand the great and incredible city of Hallandale Beach, one that has gone from being a small farming community to a mini-metropolis, the reader must first imagine what it was like when the then-unnamed site was barely a wide spot in the road. The only problem with that comment and thought, of course, is that even if it was just a wide spot, the so-called road was nothing more than a military trail, about wide enough for a cart and horse, with vegetation constantly encroaching on the pathway.

To no small extent, the concept of a group of people forming a village or town at almost any point on the east coast of Florida did not—and could not—begin without the coming of the railroad, and in the case of the place that would eventually be Hallandale Beach, that railroad was the legendary Florida East Coast (FEC) Railway. Its builder was none other than the man whose name would eventually be the single most important—and most revered—in the history of the Sunshine State: Henry M. Flagler.

Once the railroad did reach the community named for one Luther Halland, the growth, slow and painful though it was, could begin. As we learn in succeeding chapters, the birth and maturation of that community, if not directly due to Henry Flagler, was certainly because of the connection of Luther Halland to and with the FEC and its management.

By 1900, there were twelve families living in the area, but the history goes back well before then. Too often, those who are unfamiliar with Dade and now Broward County history are fond of making statements to the effect that "there's no history here—the place is too new!" so they are usually shocked to learn that the great savanna that was South Florida centuries ago was home to a rich panoply of life, both human and animal. It was in this area, according to former Miami-Dade County archaeologist Dr. Robert Carr, a resident of Broward County and the man who is considered the premier archaeology consultant in Florida, that mastodons, giant sloths, saber-toothed tigers and pre-Indian humans roamed.

Eventually, they would all go to their respective rewards as they passed along the timeline of history to be replaced by the first of the Indian tribes known to have roamed the area, the Timucuans. That tribe would be replaced by the Calusa and then the Tequesta tribes. Finally, having been pushed farther and farther south through the three Seminole wars of the nineteenth century, the Seminole and Miccosukee tribes would be the Native Americans who would be representative of all of their predecessors.

The Seminoles roamed the southeastern section of Florida, keeping mostly to themselves and staying "out of sight" by living, for the most part, in the Everglades. However, they did hunt and fish in the area that someday would be known as Hallandale. Though their settlements were inland, they harvested the coontie root, which, though poisonous when taken from the ground, could be pulverized and boiled to form starch, which they used, along with animal skins, for trade with the early white settlers.

Essentially, Hallandale began as a farming community and that was, for a good few years, its raison d'être, its reason for being. Tomatoes and pineapple predominated, although citrus was certainly another important crop. The accounts of early settlers note that Hallandale, in the beginning, was truly a "one-horse" town, that appellation not necessarily being anything but truthful, for, as was recorded in several early diaries, there was indeed one—and only one—horse, he or she being shared by the several farmers and used by each in turn as necessary for plowing. Perhaps the best part of this hard-to-believe yet absolutely true tale is the fact that a shotgun (same, apparently, purchased by the farmers who shared the horse!) would be attached to the plow whenever that implement was used for its intended purpose. And the purpose of the shotgun? It was absolutely necessary for the protection of the horse and its farmer-owners, for the entire territory was rattlesnake country, and the farm community could not take the chance of having their one beast of burden bitten by a varmint, which would, of course, result in certain death.

Hallandale would grow, though, and because of the then-new passenger train service it was no longer necessary to walk or go by buckboard or stagecoach to Fort Lauderdale, West Palm Beach or Miami (a stage line operated from Jupiter to Lemon City, which is now referred to as "Little Haiti," as early as the late 1880s), all of which were in then Dade County. But even with the coming of the railroad, settlers often remarked on the proximity of "wildcats" that prowled the Everglades, which were then much closer to the FEC tracks. (In reality, it is quite likely that what were referred to as "wildcats" were actually Florida panthers, though at the time, no distinction was made.)

The first post office was opened in 1898, by which time the Halland Colony was being shown on some of the Dade County maps as "Hallandale." The first school opened in 1904 and was the proverbial "one-room school." Ten children were enrolled in grades one through eight, and the building was a blessing for the town, as prior to that the children had to take the train to schools in Ojus, Fulford (now North Miami Beach) or Fort Lauderdale.

The school was destroyed by the 1910 hurricane, following which the county (Dade until 1915) built a two-room schoolhouse, which was also used as the parish hall for the Bethlehem Lutheran Church. In 1902, the first black church—Greater Ward AME Church—opened its doors. It is now located at 900 Northwest Sixth Avenue. Seven years later, Ebenezer Missionary Baptist opened for the first time at what would become 816 Northwest First Avenue, and both churches remain pillars of the community, with the latter church being named a historic site in March 2010. In 1912, the Shustrum family brought the first automobile into the town, but there appeared to be little interest in such a small community in starting a trend, and by 1914, Hallandale could boast of only two autos resident in the town.

Through World War I and the boom years of the 1920s, the town prospered, so much so that in the peak year of the boom, 1926, Joseph Young, developer of Hollywood, annexed the area, a move that would only last for a bit more than a year, as Young would go bankrupt in "the bust" that followed the great boom. Hallandale would move to become an incorporated town, and in May 1927, the state legislature would grant the request. The 1,500 residents were responsible for their own fate and destiny from then on.

On December 12, 1934, Hollywood Greyhound Track (today's Mardi Gras Casino and Racing) opened for the first time, and five years later, in 1939, Jack Horning's Gulfstream Park opened briefly to huge crowds. For whatever reason, Horning chose to open in competition with the legendary Hialeah Race Track, and after four days of racing, having run out of money, the track closed down and was shuttered for five years. In 1944, toward the end of World War II, Gulfstream was taken over by Jimmy Donn Sr., and the rest, as they say, "is history."

In 1947, the town reincorporated to become the city of Hallandale, at which time the city limits were expanded east from U.S. 1 (Federal Highway) to the Atlantic Ocean. In 1953, the commission–city manager form of government was adopted. In August 1999, recognizing the importance of having a city name that encompassed an area that included magnificent beachfront property, the commission voted unanimously to officially change the name of the city to Hallandale Beach, a name that reflects the fact that this great city has been, for more than ninety years, Broward County's city of choice.

Chapter 1

Henry Flagler, James Ingraham and Luther Halland

In order to understand the development of the east coast of Florida, one must recognize that although development most likely would have eventually occurred, it would have been long delayed without the arrival of one man: Henry Morrison Flagler.

Because his first wife was ill with consumption (a general term used before the invention of X-rays and relating to any disease in or emanating from the chest) due to the long and harsh northern winters, Flagler, one of the three founders of Standard Oil, left Cleveland early in the winter of 1878 and ventured to the wilds of Jacksonville. Not too many years previously, the city had its name changed from the wonderfully descriptive "Cow Ford." That moniker was appropriate, as the St. Johns River was shallow enough at one point for cows to ford the river.

Though Flagler was neither pleased with the city nor particularly impressed with its accommodations (or lack thereof), his wife, Mary, improved markedly. Because Mary's illness had become more severe, the Flaglers returned to Florida in 1881 but stayed in Orange Park, just to the south and west of Jacksonville, in Clay County. Orange Park was so named because, at the time, it was the point at which Florida's citrus belt began.

Mary died in 1883, and that winter Henry remarried. His second wife was Ida Alice Shourds, who was Mary's nurse and who would, within just a few years, succumb to mental illness, the name of the affliction today being bipolar disorder. In any event, the Flaglers traveled to St. Augustine for their honeymoon, and Henry fell in love with the town. The rest, as they say, is history, and through a series of confluences and coincidences, Henry Flagler would develop Florida's east coast with a chain of fine hotels stretching from Atlantic Beach, east of Jacksonville, to Key West, including two in the Bahamas. Along with the hotels, he incorporated several land companies, two steamship companies and the Florida East Coast Railway, which, in January 1912, would carry Mr. Flagler, James E. Ingraham, Joseph R. Parrott and other individuals now famous in Florida history on the first train to arrive in the island city.

The story of how Mr. Flagler was enticed to extend the railroad from West Palm Beach to the shores of Biscayne Bay (all, at the time, within Dade County) is the stuff of legend and does not need retelling here, except to note that it did *not* occur because Julia Tuttle, "the mother of Miami" and the first woman in America to found a city, "sent him some orange blossoms." That is a fable that, if not totally and completely debunked by now, certainly needs to be, for the facts bear no resemblance to the fairy tale that, while certainly a great marketing gimmick, has no relationship to the truth.

Following the great freezes that destroyed so much of Florida's truck (produce) and citrus in December 1894 and January and February 1895, Mrs. Tuttle asked Mr. Flagler to come and see for himself that the area that would someday be called "Miami" was untouched by the terrible freezes. Rather than make the trek into the wilderness himself, Mr. Flagler sent Mr. Ingraham and Mr. Parrott to examine Mrs. Tuttle's claims. Upon their return to St. Augustine, the company headquarters, Flagler learned that Julia was, indeed, telling the truth, whereupon he sent her a telegram in which he asked, "Madam: What is it that you propose?"

Mrs. Tuttle responded quickly: "If you will extend your railroad to the shores of Biscayne Bay, and build one of your great hotels, I will give you half of my holdings north of the river plus fifty acres for shops and yards and Mr. Brickell [William Brickell, another of Miami's pioneers] will give you half of his holdings south of the river," which, of course, refers to the Miami River. With that, a deal was struck, agreement was reached and contracts were signed. Early in 1895, construction began at West Palm Beach as the still-named Jacksonville, St. Augustine and Indian River Railway assembled men, machinery and construction materials for the task of building a railroad sixty-six miles through the South Florida underbrush to the north bank of the Miami River.

Flagler quickly recognized the value of the land to farmers, merchants and settlers, and Mr. Ingraham, as the land commissioner for the Flagler enterprises, and Mr. Parrott, as railroad vice-president, worked arduously and diligently to increase "immigration," which, at the time, meant the bringing of new arrivals from inside or outside America to Florida's east coast.

As luck would have it, the railroad, shortly after its extension to Miami was completed, had settled a group of Danish farmers along the track in the rich farming country above what would become Hollywood and below what was already, at the time, known as Fort Lauderdale. The name of the new settlement? Dania.

Incredibly, Mr. Ingraham's sister had married Luther Halland, whose father was a Lutheran minister in Stanton, Iowa. Ingraham explained to Halland what the railroad was doing and what they needed. Ingraham then hired him to bring Swedish farmers to a new settlement not too far south of Dania, that new settlement to be named "Halland" in Luther's honor. Halland was quite successful at the task to which he was assigned, and in 1898, he departed the tiny village, not returning until 1911.

In January 1898, the first land plats were filed and several areas subdivided into home lots. The original surveyor was William C. Valentine, first postmaster of Fort Lauderdale. According to several sources, the early enticement for purchase of land was an offer of a free lot in the "town section" if one bought an outlying parcel. The first buyer was a New York City widow, Matilda Gieges, who took possession of a spot of high ground known as a hammock in what today is north Miami-Dade County, along the west bank of Snake Creek. In addition to the land, though, Matilda, with her sons, Henry and August, assumed operation of a rooming house that had been built by the land company on Halland Avenue. Eventually, George Ericsson's wife would take over management of the rooming house.

The exact date of the opening of the depot to serve the new town is not known, but fortunately, through arduous examination of early FEC passenger timetables, it is apparent that the station was opened for public use some time after February 1897 and by or before February 1899. The author's collection of FEC timetables from that period has a two-year gap, as noted above; hence, it is difficult to ascertain the exact day on which the first train stopped to pick up or drop off passengers in the new town.

Upon his return in 1911, Halland, who had founded the village's first trading post, which bore his name, and who was the town's first postmaster, was astounded by the growth of both the trading post and of the town, the name of which had, some years before, had the letters "ale" added to its name. Hence, Hallandale began its rise to regional and national prominence.

There were, of course, other prominent early names, including George Ericsson, who followed Halland as postmaster; Edwin Anderson, who arrived in 1901 and who recalled going to Miami, "where a room overnight cost 25 cents and a good meal the same"; and Frank Curci, from France, whose family is still active in Hallandale business and politics as this book is being written.

By 1900, there were still only twelve families living in the town: seven were Swedish, three English and two black, or "negro," as shown on the rolls at the time. Although the town, following the southern pattern, would be segregated quite early, with the blacks settling north of Northwest Third Street, there appears to have been minimal intentional separation of the races, which was likely due to the diverse origin of the original settlers and the fact that all were dependent upon one another, regardless or race or religion, in order to assure their mutual success. It was from that slow but strongly based start that the town began its growth.

He was, indeed, "Our Founder," and were it not for Henry M. Flagler, great cities such as Hallandale Beach, a direct result of Flagler's extension of the railroad to Miami, might never have come into existence.

Standing directly behind Mr. Flagler, wearing a straw hat, *center*, and who is being welcomed to Key West by Admiral of the Port Young, is James E. Ingraham, the Flagler System's land commissioner and longtime Flagler friend and confidante. It was Ingraham who brought Luther Halland to South Florida.

The contract between Mr. Flagler, Julia Tuttle and William Brickell, extending the railroad to Miami, included an agreement whereby the FEC Hotel Company would build one of its great hotels on the shores of Biscayne Bay. Named the Royal Palm, that stately edifice is shown here in all its circa 1912 glory.

While this image shows the Ojus depot, which was the next station south of Hallandale, the station's construction and appearance is nearly identical to Hallandale's original FEC station. Although the exact date remains unknown, Hallandale's depot was opened after February 1897 but before February 1899.

Although this long-ago FEC engine crew is unidentified, we do know that 4-6-0 type number 40 hauled passenger trains through Hallandale beginning shortly after it was received from the builder, Baldwin Locomotive Works, in 1902. The 40 would continue in main-line service until replaced by larger engines following World War I.

FEC 4-6-2 number 61 was a 4-6-2 type of steam locomotive, and when it and others of the same wheel arrangement replaced engines such as number 40, train speeds were increased, and the travel time between Jacksonville and Miami reduced accordingly.

The original Curci home was in the vicinity of Southwest Fifth Street and Dixie Highway. Jim Curci's grandfather, Frank A. Curci, is seated on the porch, while Mary and Rosalie are shown in the picture. Rosina Curci, Jim's grandmother, is standing next to the house and holding her son, John P. Curci. *Courtesy Jim Curci.*

A very early Curci family photograph shows Rosina Curci (center) with Frank Curci at right and two of their eleven children. According to Jim Curci, Frank first arrived in Hallandale as early as 1905. *Courtesy Jim Curci.*

This and next page: Although the misguided attempts at "draining the Everglades" by Governor Broward were less than successful, the Hallandale area remained mostly fertile growing ground. The coconut tree, date palm and grapefruit tree shown here are perfect examples of the crop production opportunities.

This page: From the time of Luther Halland's arrival until the early 1950s, the Hallandale area, still suburban if not rural, was a rich breeding ground for both rattlesnakes and alligators, the latter moving slowly to the west as homes and businesses encroached more and more deeply into the Everglades, which, at the turn of the twentieth century, came well east of today's U.S. 441/State Road 7.

Rosina Curci enjoys the sun at the Curci home, which is now a historic landmark, with son Frank Jr. *Courtesy Jim Curci.*

Hallandale was, indeed, farm country, and several families had their own milk cows. In this incredibly rare view, Rosina Curci is hard at work milking the family's bovine. *Courtesy Jim Curci.*

The Curci family is shown "on the farm," complete with a flock of chickens in the foreground. Frank is leaning against the horse, and Rosina is in the wagon with five of their eleven children, circa 1911–12. *Courtesy Jim Curci.*

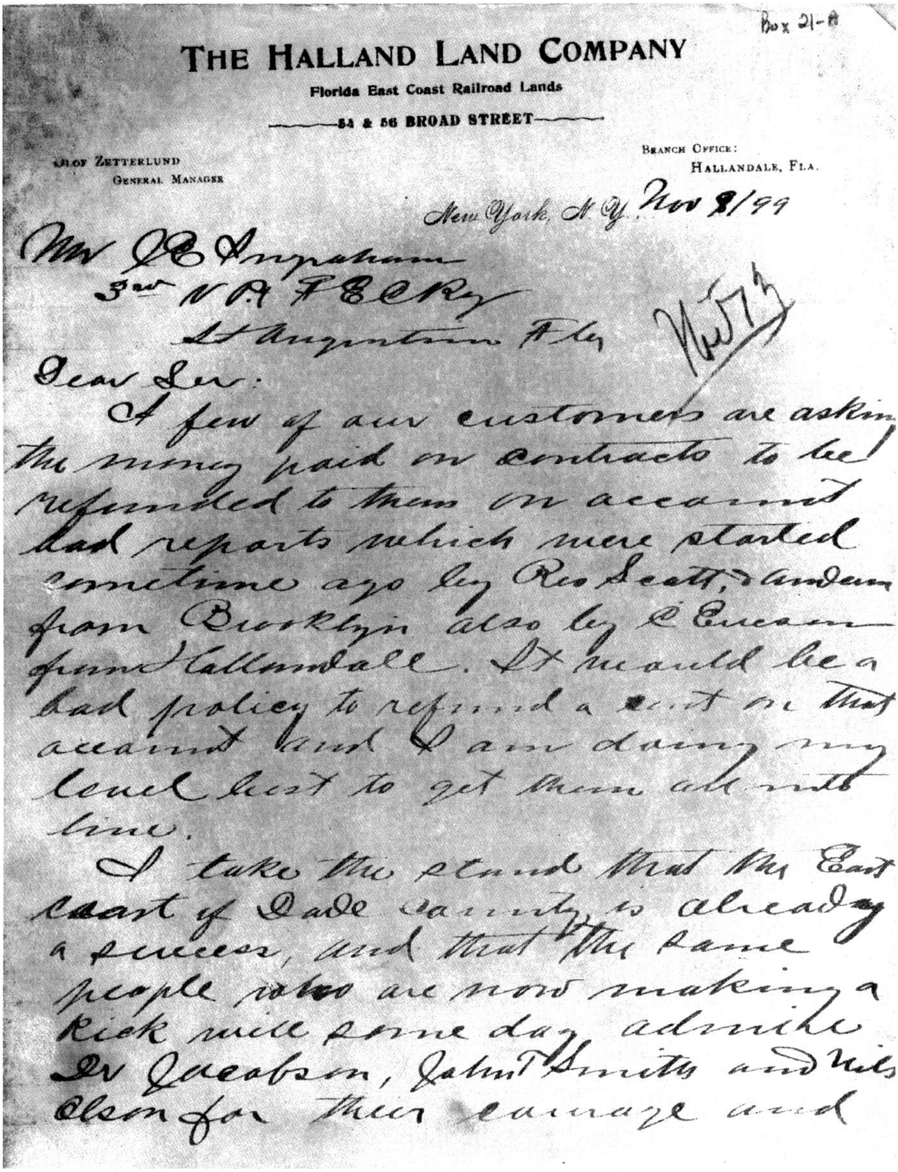

Box 21-B

THE HALLAND LAND COMPANY

Florida East Coast Railroad Lands

54 & 56 BROAD STREET

OLOF ZETTERLUND
GENERAL MANAGER

BRANCH OFFICE:
HALLANDALE, FLA.

New York, N.Y. Nov 9/99

Mr J.E. Ingraham
3rd V.P. F.E.C.Ry
St Augustine Fla

Dear Sir:

A few of our customers are asking the money paid on contracts to be refunded to them on account bad reports which were started sometime ago by Rev Scott, a man from Brooklyn also by C Encson from Hallandale. It would be a bad policy to refund a cent on that account and I am doing my level best to get them all into line.

I take the stand that the East coast of Dade county is already a success, and that the same people who are now making a kick will some day admire Dr Jacobson, John Smith and Nils Olson for their courage and

An incredible piece, this letter from and signed by Olof Zetterlund as general manager of the Halland Land Company, with offices on Broad Street in New York City, was sent to FEC vice-president James E. Ingraham on November 9, 1899. *Courtesy Vice-mayor Bill Julian.*

Chapter 2
It Grew Slowly—But It Grew!

Although, as noted in the introduction, Dade County maps were showing a community named "Hallandale" as early as 1898, the name of the Halland Land Company appears in advertising for the proposed colony in 1897. With the aid of a Swedish immigrant by the name of Olof Zetterlund, Halland went to work, traveling to Sweden and widely disseminating brochures, circulars and flyers advertising a new Swedish colony in the southeast part of Florida.

The ads proclaimed that, in that region, "the grower is safe from… frost" and went on to advise interested parties that the land was not only excellent for growing but that it was for sale at "cheap prices and on easy terms." Meantime, Halland, working with the Clyde Steamship Company, arranged for a tour of the property via one of that company's new vessels departing from New York on March 30, 1897. Although the advertising was both strong and persuasive, the new community began slowly and today one might be tempted to use the term "haltingly."

Bill McGoun, in his 1976 history of Hallandale, wrote that while the sand was originally moist enough for farming and the marl even moister, all that would change when Napoleon Bonaparte Broward became governor in 1905, bandying about his grandiose plans to "drain the Everglades to create a great growing district." The project, while apparently well intentioned, had the effect, with the digging of the drainage canals, of drying out the western side of the area's rich soil, making it less than desirable for farming.

Slowly but surely, though, immigration continued, and settlers, attracted by the weather as well as the opportunities for planting using well water or irrigation, trickled in. The kindly trade winds were, unfortunately, disturbed by the 1906 hurricane, the first recorded in central Dade County. There were unsubstantiated reports that during the hurricane, the hotel owned by the Larson family was tilted to a twenty-five-degree angle but that after the eye passed the back winds of the 'cane straightened the building! Far fetched? Indeed, but it's part of Hallandale Beach's lore and legend.

Hurricanes would become affairs of note in the town when, in 1910, that year's hurricane (they would not be named until the late 1950s) destroyed the school building. However, several other events that year attested to the slow but steady growth: Carl Palmquist graciously donated the land near the depot upon which the Community Meeting House was built (in 1914 it became the Union Community Church), and the road to Dania was covered with rock and steamrolled so that one could actually drive between the two communities without becoming bogged down in the muck generated in wet weather on the former trail-turned-roadway or covered with dust in the dry season.

One of the major contributors to the local economy in those fragile early years was the Flave Fruit Company, which encouraged and worked with the pineapple growers. Hallandale was also a major tomato-growing area, and in the tens and teens there were fourteen produce and citrus packinghouses in the town. Among the most significant of the growers and packers were Buck Schaffer's American Fruit Company, which used the name Blue Goose Packing House; H.C. "Heinie" Schwartz's operation, which used his family name; and the Florida East Coast Growers Association, which operated Barnett & Rogers, probably the largest of the tomato packers.

In 1909, Palm Beach County, which at the time of secession from Dade would include both what would later become Martin County as well as the northern part of the future Broward County, was separated from Dade County by the state legislature. For a number of reasons, including the fact that transportation by road from much of northern Dade County to downtown Miami (the county seat) required almost a full day of travel and the fact that the northern section of the county had voted itself "dry," banning alcoholic beverages in the county, residents of the southern part of Dade County voted happily to rid themselves of the north end troublemakers and in 1915 supported the creation of a new county. Florida's fifty-first county, named Broward, would take back the southernmost part of Palm Beach County and would have its southernmost corporate limit delineated at the point at which Hallandale Beach and Aventura meet today, essentially divided by

Gulfstream Race Track and Casino, although a small part of the land of that great contributor to Hallandale Beach's economy remains in today's Miami-Dade County.

Although a school existed in Hallandale, high schoolers had to travel to Fort Lauderdale and later to Dania or Hollywood. Fort Lauderdale High School's class of 1916 graduated three young ladies from Hallandale: Arva Hedrick, Marguerite Larson and Edith Palmquist. Several years later, though, with the opening of Dania High School, Hallandale's high school teenagers would not have to travel as far to complete their secondary school education. In that same year (1916), the first black school, with two rooms and teaching of grades one through eight, opened at 112 Northwest Ninth Street in a building that survived until 1975.

As the community grew, so too did the need for houses of worship. Bethlehem Lutheran, which was organized in 1906, was followed by Ebenezer Baptist, St. Ann's Episcopal and Union Congregational, with no few families participating in and at more than one church due to, as McGoun noted, "the small population of the town and the lack of social outlets."

The Seminole Indians were also part of the pre- and early 1920s in Hallandale, particularly one unique individual named "Shirt-Tail Charlie," who supposedly was a tribal outcast, the reason for that never having been explained. Charlie, who died in the mid- to late 1920s, was a familiar sight in early Hallandale and was known to almost all of the settlers. Most of the Seminoles did not come in to Hallandale at all, it not being a trading post. However, in the late tens or early teen years of the twentieth century, a family of western Indians, the tribe unknown today, did live on Northwest Second Avenue.

Although the beachfront was known to most of the early Hallandallians, it was strictly thought of as a place of and for recreation, as getting there required the use of a rowboat to cross the canal (later the Intracoastal Waterway) until 1917, when the first bridge was put in place. That years-long effort was the culmination of work begun by Thomas B. Hamilton as early as 1914. Hamilton, building an east–west canal and using the fill for the eastward extension of Halland Avenue (the first Beach Boulevard), planned to plat and sell oceanfront land for use as homesites. After a lengthy series of meetings, disagreements, agreements, contracts, promises and Hamilton's donation of beachfront land for use as a park, the bridge was approved and erected.

In 1917, the White Star Auto Line, an early Florida intra-state bus operator, began service between Miami and West Palm Beach at rates that the company claimed matched the FEC's tariff. The construction between Chicago and Miami of the Dixie Highway, being promoted by Miami

Beach's builder, Carl G. Fisher, had very little effect on Hallandale, but with the coming of World War I and its conclusion, the turn of the decade would bring changes to Florida's Gold Coast—including Hallandale—that, just a few years previously, would have been unimaginable.

This page: It was early in the teens when Thomas B. Hamilton first attempted to convince government and private investors of the idea of a causeway and bridge over to the beach side. His attempts finally paid off in 1917 with the opening of the first bridge across the canal (later Intracoastal Waterway). The arduous work of digging and filling is shown here.

This page: Hallandale Elementary School, circa 1920–22. The building was made of concrete and had large windows to allow the Florida sunshine to pour into the classrooms. Built on the later site of Hallandale City Hall, the building burned in the 1930s. *CoHB.*

Commencement Exercises

of the

DANIA HIGH SCHOOL

HIGH SCHOOL AUDITORIUM

Thursday Evening, June 6th, 1929
Eight P. M.

Hallandale's students of high school age attended Dania High School in the 1920s and early 1930s. The 1929 commencement exercises program and list of graduates included a number of Hallandallians including, among others, Alvin Gieges and Guilda Ingalls. *CoHB*.

The home of J.W. Moffitt. Built circa 1917 and shown in 1976, it has been preserved by the city and now holds historic structure status. Currently being restored, it is next to the Curci home, which is also under restoration. *CoHB.*

Union Congregational Church was one of the city's pioneer houses of worship, beginning life as the Community Meeting House and becoming a church in 1914. Photographed by Walter Gray of Hollywood, and shown here in 1951, the building looked very much like it did when it first became a church. *CoHB.*

UNION CONGREGATIONAL CHURCH

Hallandale, Florida

Rev. Luther C. Pierce, Pastor

Church Directory

1970

In 1970, celebrating its fifty-sixth anniversary, the church published this well-illustrated members and officers directory. *CoHB.*

Rosalie Curci Kenyon, one of Frank's daughters, was a stunning beauty. Shown here in the late 1920s, she would later become the hat check girl at the famous La Boheme, one of Hallandale's several casinos, which operated in the 1930s and 1940s. *Courtesy Jim Curci.*

Frank Curci, a member of the Florida National Guard, stands at attention as he guards a troop train that was parked on an FEC siding just south of the Hallandale depot. *CoHB*.

This page: Hallandale pioneer August F. Gieges is shown in a dapper pose with tie, jacket and hat, and, *below*, with his family on the beach at Hallandale. *CoHB*.

Chapter 3

Joseph Young, Hollywood and the Disasters of 1926

With the end of World War I, a general euphoria descended on the entire nation. Business, though slightly down following the war's end, would begin to increase as the country entered a new era and decade: the 1920s.

Hallandale, at that point, was still little more than a name on a map, known only for tomato and pineapple farms and completely overshadowed by the towns and cities to the north and south of it, from Fulford (North Miami Beach) and Ojus in Dade County to Dania, Fort Lauderdale and Pompano Beach in what had been Broward County since 1915.

Hallandale was simply the name of a place that had as its claim to fame fourteen fruit and vegetable packinghouses. Nobody at that juncture of history could have any idea of or foresee what would occur beginning in 1921, when the most incredible and unbridled growth in the nation's history would sweep much of coastal Florida but would have as its epicenter the gold coast, that region on Florida's east coast between West Palm Beach and Coral Gables.

That growth began slowly, almost casually, as Carl Fisher in Miami Beach and George Merrick in what would become Coral Gables began the work that would eventually create two of America's most famous cities. But as the decade moved forward, more and more developers and entrepreneurs, attracted by the sun, the sand, the weather, the money-making potential and the bathing beauties known as "cheesecake," set up shop in Dade and Broward Counties.

Many of the names have developed a world-class cachet, and that lofty bracket includes one Joseph Young. Coming from California in 1920, he would purchase a one-square-mile tract of land just north of the approximate boundaries of Hallandale, which, at that time, was not an incorporated municipality but was, rather, simply a community of people with mostly like interests.

Because of the national (well, almost national, as the huge bulk of said promotion was done from Kansas City east, the early promoters believing that there was little interest in coming to Florida if one lived west of that imaginary line of demarcation, those inhabiting that vast region preferring, it was believed at the time, the golden state of California) advertising and publicity being done by, among others, the Florida East Coast Railway and many of the cities in the tri-county area, directed at those who wished to live, farm, open businesses or vacation on the gold coast, Florida was perceived as the "Fountain of Youth" and as a place where anything was possible, land could be purchased for a song and the streets were (symbolically) paved with gold. Joseph Young was one who believed that all of those things were true.

Although McGoun stated that Young "moved in" in 1921, an article written by Jack R. Adams and titled "Hallandale's History" appeared in the Winter–Spring 1993 *Broward Legacy*, published by the Broward County Historical Commission, which, along with several other sources, made it clear that Young did arrive in 1920, following which he purchased the one square mile of land noted above. He would begin land development operations of the area that he named "Hollywood-by-the-Sea" in 1921, surveying, platting and clearing the land for his proposed city. Along with other South Florida promoters—including, among others, Carl Fisher, George Merrick, Harvey Baker Graves (Sunny Isles), Ellen Spears Harris and Hugh Anderson (Miami Shores) and Fulford-by-the Sea's (later North Miami Beach) Merle Tebbetts—Young provided free transportation from many parts of the country, along with free meals, housing and entertainment to prospective buyers of his development.

Acquiring 4,723 acres on the mainland and 563 acres of beachfront, Young built a garage (for his construction vehicles), an administration building and a marvelous hostelry that, at the time, was the equal of the Flagler System resorts in Palm Beach and Miami. Although sounding far-fetched, several sources stated that "Hollywood's population was 30,000 by 1925," and if that was correct, it was the largest city in Broward County at the time. All of that growth attracted the attention of Hallandale's residents, and on January 15, 1926, a petition signed by a majority of the unincorporated area's property owners was presented to the Hollywood City Commission (which, at that point, had been in existence for less than two months!) requesting inclusion in the great and growing city just north of them. The petition was approved, and Hallandale became a part of Hollywood-by-the-Sea, a marriage that would end in divorce barely more than a year later.

And what caused the breakup? The five terrible events of 1926, beginning with the capsizing of the five-masted Danish schooner *Prinz Valdemar* in the turning basin of the Miami harbor, which blocked all ships from entering or leaving the port, and culminating with the horrific hurricane of September 17 and 18, 1926, the damage from which was not equaled in South Florida until Hurricane Andrew in August 1992.

Along with Merrick, Tebbetts, Spears Harris and Anderson, who had gone bankrupt following the hurricane, Young, facing immense rebuilding costs coupled with innumerable defaults by lot, home and property buyers, was on the verge of financial disaster. Even until his death in 1934, Young could not bring himself to face the fact that, with Hollywood in ruins, on the brink of foreclosure by banks and threats of government seizure of his assets, he was finished.

The Hallandallians, recognizing their potential liabilities in the event of a default by Young, who was being hounded by creditors and served with lawsuits on an almost daily basis, appeared before the Hollywood City Commission on November 26, 1926, just two months after the storm, and asked to be separated (de-annexed) from and by the city. In March 1927, the request was approved, and a group of Hallandale residents, led by J.W. Moffitt Sr., presented the state legislature with a petition for incorporation as a town, same being quickly approved by that august body. But to be certain that the Hallandale folks would never be burdened with Young's and Hollywood's debts, the legislature passed a companion bill that declared that Hallandale had never been a part of Hollywood (similar to a marriage annulment) and assuring that the former would never be assessed for the latter's indebtedness, thereby allowing Hallandale to come into existence as a town debt-free.

On May 14, 1927, Hallandale's voters ratified the charter by an overwhelming vote of 229 to 21, and to officially begin the town's life, the charter named Oliver L. White as mayor and Moffitt as president of the town council, each with two-year terms.

The first council, besides Moffitt, included Charles Ericsson, C.E. Ingalls, Olof Zetterlund (it was he who was general manager of the Halland Land Company) and Henry L. Gieges, the same two-year terms applying to them. The council appointed John Fenn as city clerk, tax appraiser and tax collector, Malcolm Sterrett as attorney and P.H. Lee as town marshal, a position equivalent to today's title of chief of police. The first town hall was a white frame building at 124 Northwest Ninth Street, and according to the *Hallandale Digest* of May 5, 1977, a tin building on Southeast Third Avenue with two lion cages inside to house prisoners served as the jail.

A new town, with a population of either just under one thousand people (*Broward Legacy* article, Winter–Spring 1993) or "only 1500 people" (McGoun) had come to life! Unfortunately, neither the article nor the book makes note of where the number came from or how it was derived, so it is likely safe to state that the actual number of residents that spring of 1927 was somewhere in between.

Hollywood Research Bulletin

Published by The Hollywood Research Bureau, H. W. Hurt, Director

Vol. 1 January 23, 1926 No. 1

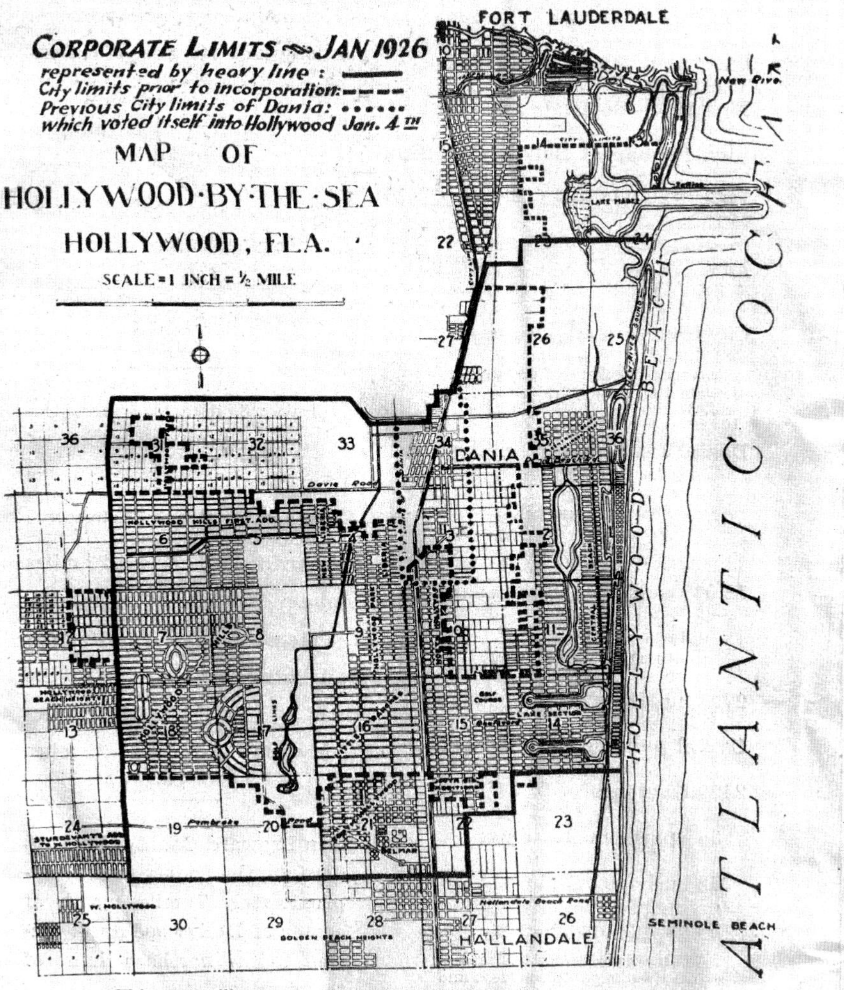

This map will prove useful in answering questions of distance as the section lines, one mile each way, are clearly shown.

Beginning on January 23, 1926, the Hollywood Research Bureau, under the direction of H.W. Hurt, began publishing the *Hollywood Research Bulletin*, a 6 1/8-inch by 9-inch four-page weekly discussion of various topics of interest to those in Joseph Young's Hollywood, which had been incorporated as a city on November 25, 1925. When this issue, volume 1, number 1, dated January 23, 1926, was published, what would later become the city of Dania was shown as part of Hollywood. Though Hallandale was partially shown, this issue had apparently gone to press too early for the community to be shown within Hollywood's corporate limits.

HOLLYWOOD By-the-Sea, FLORIDA

RELIGIOUS DIRECTORY OF HOLLYWOOD

Church	Organized	Pastor
Baptist	**Jan., 1926**	**Rev. J. L. Evans**

Baptist Church—Meets in Public School Building; Services, 11 A. M.-7:30 P. M.; Sunday School, 9:45 A. M.; Membership, 60; Average Attendance, 60.

Catholic .... **1924** .... **Rev. Father Mullaly**
Catholic Church—Meets in Hollywood Theatre; Mass, 8:30 A. M.; Sunday School, 9:30 A. M.; Average Attendance, 500.

Lutheran .... **Jan., 1926** .... **Rev. J. L. Younce**
Lutheran Church—Meets in Hippodrome Theatre; Services, 11 A. M.; Sunday School, 10 A. M.; Membership, 27; Average Attendance, 90.

Methodist .... **March, 1924** .... **Dr. J. H. Mather**
Methodist Church—Church, East Dixie and Van Buren; Services, 11 A. M.-8 P. M.; Sunday School, 9:45 A. M.; Young People's Meeting, 7 P. M.; Membership, 150; Average Attendance, 425.

Presbyterian .... **April, 1925** .... **Dr. W. J. Garrison**
Presbyterian Church—Meets in Hollywood Theatre; Services, 11 A. M.; Membership, 96; Average Attendance, 300.

DANIA SECTION

Methodist .... **1912** .... **Rev. A. H. Moore**
Methodist Church—Meets in M. E. Church; 11 A. M.-7:30 P. M.; Sunday School 10 A. M.; Epworth League, 6:45 P. M.; Membership, 170; Attendance, 120.

Baptist .... **1920** .... **Rev. P. T. Taylor**
Baptist Church—Meets in First Baptist Church; 11 A. M.-7:30 P. M.; Sunday School 10 A. M.; Attendance, about 300; Membership, approximately 500; Prayer Meeting Wednesday, 6:30 P. M.; B. Y. P. U., Sunday, 6:30 P. M.

HALLANDALE SECTION

Lutheran .... **1912** .... **Rev. Paul V. Nelson**
Lutheran Church—Meets in Church building; Serices, 11 A. M.-7:30 P. M.; Sunday School, 10 A. M.; Membership, 55.

Union Church .... **Rev. Garrison 1st Sunday (Presby.)**
Rev. Kimes 2nd-3rd Sundays (Bap.)
Rev. York 4th Sunday (Methodist)

Union Church—Meets in Church building; Services, 11 A. M.-7:30 P. M.; Sunday School, 10 A. M.; three bodies average total 80.

NOTE:—A Christian Church is to be organized soon.

The Catholic Church is preparing a large building program on Block 131—Hollywood Hills.

The Baptist congregation reports progress on their building fund. Building addition to Dania church.

The Methodist Community Church has begun a quiet campaign to pay for and complete their church building.

According to the U. S. Census, considerably more than half of the population are non-church-members.

In Florida the Baptists outnumber the Methodists slightly. Together they represent over three-fourths of the total. Then follow in sequence—Roman Catholic, Protestant Episcopal, Presbyterian, Disciples, Congregationalists, Adventists, etc.

Although Hallandale became part of Hollywood in January, the first issue of the *Hollywood Research Bulletin* to include any indication that Hallandale was part of the city was in volume 1, number 7, dated March 6, 1926. The back cover of that issue, shown here, presents a religious directory of Hollywood and includes both the Dania and Hallandale sections. It can be noted that both the Lutheran Church and the Union Church were in existence and that "a Christian Church is to be organized soon."

Hollywood's Young-era post office, likely built by the developer.

First known as the Hollywood Hotel, the hostelry would shortly have the name "Beach" added and would become one of the most desirable destinations on the gold coast. A full frontal view, taken shortly after completion, is shown here.

Above: A close-up of the hotel, this view looking south, gives an idea of the expansiveness of the property.

Left: Regretfully, there is no known record nor is there a complete set of the beautiful, full-color ads that the Hollywood-by-the-Sea Company placed in newspapers and magazines throughout America. Fortunately, a good few of them have been saved by collectors, this piece featuring Hollywood Boulevard at top center a prime example.

This page: Two pictures taken shortly after the 1926 hurricane strongly portray the damage done by the storm. Although Hallandale and Hollywood were north of the Miami epicenter, the powerful storm's effects were felt well north of Fort Lauderdale. Hollywood's Ford garage and First ME Church both sustained severe damage.

A Texaco oil tanker's crew looks over the terrible damage caused by the storm, which totally destroyed Hallandale's first filling station. The Texaco-logoed pylons, at center of photo, just behind the truck, are the only remaining evidence that the property was once the Hallandale Garage. *Courtesy Jim Curci.*

The resiliency of what would become a great and famous city is exemplified by the former Gieges Building, shown circa 1964 at Dixie Highway and Southwest Fifth Street. Surviving every hurricane that has struck the town and then the city, the building is one of several surviving structures dating back to Hallandale's earliest years. On the top center, the date has been cemented over but the façade is still as it was at the time the building was completed. Having gone through several incarnations, it is now an office building for Southern Limousine Services. *Courtesy the Donn family.*

In concluding this chapter, it is a privilege to present, for only the second time ever known to have been published, this incredible image, provided by Denyse Cunningham, curator of the Broward County Historical Commission and Museum. This photograph, taken by an unknown lensman, was made on May 14, 1927, and shows not only the ballot box where the votes were cast to determine the fate of the Hallandale community but, in addition, several of Hallandale's legendary pioneers. Frank Curci is seated, while standing, *from left to right*, are Mickey Curci, Donald Curci, August Gieges, Henry Gieges and John Hart. The vote count was 229 for incorporation as a town, with 21 opposed. *BCHC.*

Chapter 4
A Town Becomes a Great City

Hallandale, as a newly incorporated municipality, extended from Moffett Street (which then went west to Dixie Highway) south to the Dade County line and from the Federal Highway area on the east to Eighth Avenue on the west. The original plans called for Hallandale to incorporate as far north as Washington Street, but compromises related to the town's separation from Hollywood and subsequent incorporation had to be agreed to, and, for the moment, Moffett Street would be the town's north boundary. Hallandale had, on May 14, 1927, few resources and perhaps even less money, but one thing was for certain: the town was now the master of its own fate and destiny.

The five terrible events of 1926, culminating with the September 17 and 18 hurricane, and which began Florida's economic downturn, were the harbinger of the Great Depression that would begin in the rest of the United States in 1929. Another hurricane, in 1928, did nothing to improve Florida's image, and investors and potential property buyers sat on their haunches, wary of anything having to do with putting money into Florida land or businesses.

There was, sadly, one other "terrible event" affecting the new town that occurred on April 28, 1928. Following a "theft of service" (refusal to pay a restaurant check) complaint, Police Chief Phillip H. Lee, who, unfortunately, was driving through the neighborhood where his murder would occur, was hailed by Broward County deputy sheriff C.M. Ingalls regarding the incident. In seeking out the perpetrator, Lee, Hallandale's first town marshal and police chief, was shot and killed. The murderer, who was hunted down and killed by a posse hastily deputized to search for the man, also shot Deputy Clyde Dixon, who died the following day. Lee, a relative of Miami police chief and later mayor and city commissioner H. Leslie Quigg, left a large family and a grieving community, the shock of Lee's killing being exacerbated when Dixon died on April 29. Both Lee and Dixon have been memorialized in the lobby of the Hallandale Beach Police Department headquarters adjacent to city hall at 400 South Federal Highway.

Hallandale's population was essentially stagnant during the 1930s while business was in a state of malaise, with little happening to improve economic conditions other than, at first, governmental actions to take over and widen the Florida Coast Line Canal and Transportation Company's East Coast Canal and create the Intracoastal Waterway while simultaneously relocating East Dixie Highway south of Beach Boulevard to create Federal Highway, which today is also known as U.S. 1.

The people of the area recognized that something had to be done to improve both the economy and opportunities for employment, and with those thoughts uppermost in their collective minds, they recognized that legalized gaming in the form of parimutuel betting had to be approved. Ratified overwhelmingly on September 8, 1934, the positive results of the referendum allowed the Hollywood Greyhound Track to begin racing operations on December 12. But the people wanted more, and several gambling casinos, not legal until 1937 and then for only two years, opened in the early 1930s, most likely as a result of and from the profits generated by bootlegging. Hallandale became, depending upon the point of view, either famous or infamous for its several wide-open casinos, including, among others, La Boheme in the Zetterlund's beachfront home, Colonial Inn (just south of Gulfstream Race Track), Hollywood Country Club and "Potatoes" Kaufman's Old Plantation, just west of the present location of the Diplomat Mall on Hallandale Beach Boulevard.

Slot machines were available in most gas stations and retail stores, but when all games of chance were outlawed by constitutional amendment in 1938 (which excluded parimutuels from the prohibition) the owners simply moved them into back rooms. In the black community, bolita, a numbers game similar to lotto, lasted long after the other forms of gaming had been forced out of existence in Florida, and it was only with the amending of the state's constitution five decades later to enable the introduction of the lottery games that bolita, which had been sold in stores and from delivery trucks, finally disappeared from the scene.

The Depression, while not an era of major construction, did see some buildings rise, most notably in the government or entertainment sectors. Of note was the then-new city hall, which, in 1941, moved from its original Northwest Ninth Street site to a brand-new single-story building at 308 South Federal Highway complete with, according to a Summer/Fall 1981 *Broward Legacy* article, "a jail (which) was constructed at the same time." In 1944, Gulfstream Race Track, closed since 1939, was reopened. Although the city did experience some growth during World War II, it remained essentially a suburban/rural community with buildings surrounded by fields, some farms and the two racetracks, the histories of which will be discussed individually in Chapters 7 and 8.

Unlike many of the surrounding Dade and Broward towns and cities, Hallandale saw little "on-the-ground" military activity during the war. Miami Beach, Miami and Fort Lauderdale, along with the Hollywood Beach Hotel, saw billeting, mess-hall operation and training on the beaches and in the cities.

At that time, with nothing other than very small "cabins" (an early variant of the later motels) or tourist courts (a slightly less rudimentary advancement, often with a swimming pool available but still "air-cooled," meaning you either had a fan or opened the windows to get some circulation!), neither of which provided the military with either the type or quantity of facilities that the various services needed for their troops, sailors or airmen and women, Hallandale was not in a position to offer services to the armed forces.

By the end of the war, Hallandale remained little more than "a wide spot in the road," the original boundaries unchanged since incorporation. The town boasted three service or filling stations, Barnett's Hardware Store and two grocery stores, with literally nothing else in the way of retail businesses. Most of the townspeople still kept horses stabled at their homes, and only the dog track—in Hallandale but with Hollywood's name on it—and Gulfstream Park, with its thoroughbred horse racing, brought a steady flow of visitors, but then only when racing was in season.

In 1947, a group led by J.W. Moffitt Jr. again approached the state legislature, but this time with a request to amend the town's charter to allow it to not only become a city but also to annex the land from Federal Highway (U.S. 1) east to the ocean. The request, though approved, gave Hollywood the land on the ocean side north of Beach Boulevard; hence, the new city was inaugurated with an oddly shaped boundary that did, however, include all of the property east of Federal Highway south to the county line, which placed Gulfstream Park inside the city limits, where it has remained since that time. In 1953, the city's charter was amended to provide for a city manager form of government, he or she to manage the city while reporting to the city commission, which had the power to hire and fire that person.

In addition to becoming a city in 1947, the new city's volunteer fire department came into existence in that year. However, with the city growing, paid driver-engineers were added on a full-time basis sometime in the 1950s, the volunteers then responding to assist the driver-engineers. Although the volunteers continued in service, the city began hiring full-time firefighters in the early 1960s, and in 1971, the department became fully paid, with volunteers assuming administrative but not firefighting or rescue tasks.

By 1950, the city's population had risen to over 3,800 but just a decade later had tripled. In 1966, Hallandale had a population of almost 21,000, and a year later another 2,000 people had become residents of the "big little city," which was booming and gaining national publicity thanks to the two racetracks. By the 2000 census, Hallandale Beach was, indeed, "big time," with a permanent population of over 44,000 and a family median income of over $37,000.

Part of a city's greatness emanates from the dedication of its citizenry and their willingness to be civic-minded and proactive in community affairs. Along with other service clubs, the Hallandale Beach Rotary has been a standout. Founded in 1957 with Henry Rensburgh Jr. as its first president, the club has been a bastion of support for the city since its formation. Today, with a who's who list of members, the club, with Maritza Velez as president, is looking forward to many more years of service.

Hallandale has, deservedly, taken its rightful place in the Florida sun, and, in the process, become a nationally known place to live, own a business, vacation in or just relax. Indeed, Hallandale Beach *is* "Broward County's City of Choice!"

Joseph W. Moffitt Jr. His father was the first president of the town council, and it was Joseph Jr. who would lead the drive to change Hallandale's corporate designation from "town" to "city." *CoHB.*

Joseph Moffitt Jr.'s daughters, Joyslyn (left) and Betty Jo (right), are enjoying their bicycles at a time when children could ride anywhere throughout the still mostly rural town with little worry about the hazards of automobile traffic. *CoHB.*

Francis C. "Biz" Bisson began his career with the City of Hallandale as a volunteer fireman and would eventually become the city's first paid fire chief. Retiring only because of ill health, "Biz" dedicated his entire working career to the city he loved. *Courtesy Kathy Bisson Cianfrani.*

Kathleen "Kathy" (left) and Alice Bisson dressed up beautifully for Hallandale's 1947 Halloween night festivities. *Courtesy Kathy Bisson Cianfrani.*

Celebrating the completion of their new building and the acceptance of Hallandale Volunteer Fire Department truck number one, a group of city officials and volunteers gather outside the new station shortly after its February 1948 opening. *CoHB.*

Although the volunteer department's beautiful Dalmatian, Noz-zel, is not shown in this picture, "Biz" Bisson (left), later to become the first full-time paid department chief, is shown with then chief Jo Jo Balvage (seated, right) greeting 1948 Fiesta Queen Joyce Lombard as she gets an up-close look at the department's first truck. *CoHB.*

The Hallandale Volunteer Fire Department refreshments committee took a moment for a group photograph prior to the building's public opening on Dedication Day, February 8, 1948. While, unhappily to report, the first names are not known, the women, all married, are, *from left*, Mrs. Donn, Placey, Schmoll, Artagus, Tice, Morrow, Paradise, Haas, Ericson, McGregor, Buford and Barlow. *CoHB.*

Eleven of Hallandale's finest, representing the city's police department, are shown in the early 1950s in a group photo. Police Chief Hugh Bush is seated second from left, while Mayor Foster Ingalls is seated second from right. The remainder of the men are unidentified, but, showing Hallandale's belief in equality and diversity even then, the force includes the city's first two black officers, B.J. Jordan and Roy Mosely. *CoHB.*

A circa 1952 Neel Photo aerial view presents an incredible panorama of a small city about to burst into full bloom as one of South Florida's most important destinations. Looking west from above the Atlantic Ocean, the through street on the left is Hallandale Beach Boulevard, in all of its two-laned glory. Gulfstream Race Track's dormitories are at center left, while the Hollywood Dog Track (which is in Hallandale) is at upper right center. Except when passing through the towns and cities, U.S. 1 was two lanes. *CoHB.*

A lower-level view, also by Neel Photo of Fort Lauderdale, was taken over Gulfstream's parking lots looking west and shows very little development. U.S. 1 runs from left to right in the lower part of the photo, and today's Flashback Diner, public library and city hall sit in a triangle shown by the road intersection of Old Federal Highway, which begins at the far right (north end) of the photo. Southeast Sixth Street is the base of the triangle. *CoHB.*

Foster Ingalls was mayor of the city from 1950 through 1958 and is shown here with his secretary, Lu Day, signing the city's municipal bonds that were issued to pay for capital improvements during his eight-year term. *Walter Gray photo; CoHB.*

The Hallandale Kiwanis Club was founded in 1948 with Mr. Ingalls as its first president. Shown here at the charter dinner are, *from left*, Ingalls, his wife Dee and H.C. "Heinie" Schwartz, who was outgoing mayor at the time this picture was taken, he having served the city in that capacity since 1944. In 1924, Schwartz's family arrived in what, three years later, formally became the town of Hallandale. *CoHB*.

This is a spectacular view, literally one of a kind, for nothing like this has ever before surfaced in any known printed or published Broward County or Hallandale Beach history: the builder of Golden Isles, "Pappy" Layne, is standing in front of the entrance arch shortly after the sales office, *at left*, had opened. The only building of note in this image is the newly

opened Diplomat in the distance on the left, allowing us to date this picture to circa 1958. A two-lane Hallandale Beach Boulevard is the street on which the CARCO truck is driving, heading east toward the beach in a one-of-a-kind, never-to-be-repeated view. *Courtesy Arthur J. Rosenberg.*

H.B. "Pappy" Layne, who built Golden Isles and, along with the Curci brothers, the Three Islands development. *Candid Art Photography photo.*

John Curci, in addition to being a great Hallandale Beach pioneer, was a proud father and grandfather and is shown here on the occasion of his seventieth birthday in 1983 with sons Jerry (left) and Jim (right) and granddaughter Crystal, in her dad's arms. *CoHB.*

This page: When the town vacated the original municipal building in 1941, it moved to a beautiful state-of-the-art facility at 308 South Dixie Highway. Both the close-up of the building and the panoramic view show the famous cannons, which were found in the ocean off Hallandale by Eddie and Dennis Pickett, Buddy Tanguay, Jack Wilson and Donny Williams. The panoramic view, with the police department located in the building, is circa 1949–50, while the close up, apparently taken after the police moved to a separate facility, appears to be circa 1961–62. The building was renovated and remodeled in 1973–74 and was eventually sold when the new government center and police headquarters was opened in 1997. *CoHB*.

Most of the Hallandale children, prior to the opening of junior high, the middle school and Hallandale Beach High, attended McNicol Junior High School (the 1960 *Hawk Times* yearbook shown here) and then South Broward High. *Courtesy Pat Saba.*

Among the Hallandallians who attended South Broward was Betty Jo Moffitt Cunningham, who graduated from the high school in 1957. *CoHB.*

Hallandale Elementary School has seen thousands of Hallandale and Hallandale Beach's children pass through its portals. *CoHB.*

Politics in Hallandale Beach, almost from day one, has always been nothing short of interesting and is usually quite exciting. In 1949, one of George Smathers's young supporters passed out campaign literature in front of city hall. *CoHB.*

One of Hallandale Beach's distinguished police chiefs, George Emmerick, who served as chief from 1965 until 1973. *CoHB.*

Hallandale Police Department
100 S.W. 4th Street
Hallandale, Florida 33009-6395

KENNETH R. WAGNER
CHIEF OF POLICE

EXECUTIVE OFFICE
TEL. 305-921-3518
EXT. 171

UNIFORM SHIELD

THE RIGHT TOP QUARTER DEPICTS A SWIMMER. THE WEATHER IN THE CITY OF HALLANDALE BEING CONDUCIVE TO YEAR ROUND SWIMMING.

THE UPPER LEFT QUARTER DEPICTS A HORSE HEAD, SIGNIFICANT OF ANNUAL GULFSTREAM TRACK THOROUGHBRED RACING.

THE LOWER RIGHT QUARTER DEPICTS A GOLFER. THE BEAUTIFUL DIPLOMAT GOLF COURSE OFFERS SUPERB GOLFING FACILITIES YEAR ROUND.

THE LOWER LEFT QUARTER DEPICTS A GREYHOUND DOG SIGNIFICANT OF DECEMBER THROUGH APRIL TRAINED GREYHOUND RACES AT THE HOLLYWOOD KENNEL CLUB IN HALLANDALE.

THIS UNIFORM SHIELD WAS INSPIRED AND DESIGNED BY A HALLANDALE POLICE OFFICER

F392802/TXTPOLIC

A patch prior to that in use today on Hallandale Beach Police uniforms is shown with department stationery explaining the four quadrants of the patch. Kenneth R. Wagner was chief of police at the time, and as the word "Beach" was added to the city's name in 1999, we know that this patch precedes that date. *Courtesy Commissioner Dorothy Ross.*

On January 31, 1984, K-9 officer Dennis White took a moment during patrol to greet *Hollywood Sun-Tattler* photographer James M. Urick. *BCHC.*

Three of the city's motorcycle officers prepare to depart the station on June 8, 1984. *CoHB.*

In June 1980, then police department employee Dorothy Ross presents Chief Richard Fox, who began his tenure as chief in 1976, with the plaque honoring him for being selected as a member of "Who's Who Among Students in American Colleges and Universities" as he was finishing his Florida International University degree. *Courtesy Commissioner Dorothy Ross.*

Fire Chief "Biz" Bisson stands proudly next to the city's new pump truck shortly after its 1970 delivery. One year later, the department was fully paid, with volunteers acting only in administrative functions. *Peter Bluesten photo, collection of CoHB.*

Above: The Hallandale Police and Fire Department building, with police cars parked in the lot. Barely visible to the left of the building is the Curci home. The building was built during the city hall remodeling project of 1973–74, and this photograph was made shortly after the building opened. *CoHB*.

Left: Longtime city attorney Quentin Long. Long came to Hallandale as a child in 1929 and served as a state attorney for Broward County. After years of service to the legal community and the city, he became chairman of Bank of Hallandale. *CoHB*.

It is September 1958, and the tug *Mary K.* is towing one of the two-lane spans of the Hallandale Beach bridge to the point in the Intracoastal Waterway where it will be temporarily reset in place to be used until the then-new bridge was completed. *CoHB.*

By 1959, the new bridge (in the background) was mostly complete, and the old bridge, with temporary paving, was in place until the new bridge was opened. *CoHB.*

Hallandale's Florida East Coast Railway station, 1920. This station, incredibly, was moved and used for other purposes, with the city now preparing to preserve it as a museum and possibly move it back to its original site on the southeast corner of Southeast First Avenue and Hallandale Beach Boulevard. *BCHC.*

This page: This is the former FEC depot today. Along with the Curci and Moffitt houses, the preserved station will be a shining example of how a caring city can protect and enshrine its glorious past. *BCHC.*

Everybody loves a parade, and this stunning float, adorned with seven of the city's beauties, was Hallandale's contribution to the 1960 Orange Bowl parade, an event that, sadly, is nothing more than a South Florida memory. *CoHB.*

Hallandale's girls have always been the county's prettiest, and here majorette Pam Wallace, photographed by John Ashcraft Jr., proves it in the December 18, 1974 Peppermint Stick parade. *BCHC.*

Congratulations Hallandale

1927 – 1977

A Slow Starter

Edwin Anderson plows his tomato field.

But Look at it Now 50 Years Later

by Betty Cochran
for TOWN TOPICS

It took 4,000 years for the area near the northern most tip of Biscayne Bay to attract settlers,

And then it wasn't until 1897 after Flagler had train service running into Miami, that the area now known as Hallandale was proclaimed by namesake Luther Halland as "a large tract of the most excellent land for growing. . ."

Halland, son of a Swedish min-

Looking east on Hallandale Beach Blvd.

TOWN TOPICS/5

In May 1977, *Town Topics*, a semi-regular local publication for and about the communities of South Broward, featured, as did the *Hallandale Digest* that same month, the city's fiftieth anniversary. The cover of the May issue of *Town Topics* is shown here. Regretfully, neither publication exists today. *BCHC.*

Though located in Hollywood, Hallandale's high schoolers, until their own public high school was built in and named for the city, attended South Broward High School, which, when opened, allowed Hallandale students to cut the trip to and from Dania High School in half.

Chapter 5
Hotels, Restaurants and Clubs

In preparing a municipal history, many authors, in (hopefully) doing the due diligence required to prepare a superior (rather than just an "adequate") history of the town or city that they are commemorating, will often find that the names and years of service of every council person, commissioner, mayor, fire chief and chief of police have been recorded but that, conversely, no amount of searching through the most arcane and obscure files and records, including newspapers and, in the case of those that are defunct, their left-behind microfilm or microfiche, can or will yield either the date of the opening of the first hospitality venue or any partial, much less complete, record of the hotels, trailer parks, restaurants and clubs that might have existed, for however briefly or lengthily, in a given locale.

In McGoun's 1976 tome, *Hallandale*, wherein he does a fine job commemorating the growing city up to that point and includes reminiscences of nineteen of the town's and city's pioneers, it should be noted that not one of them, in their remembrances, communicated any information regarding hostelries or dining/drinking establishments other than the casinos, and for that, more is the pity. In fact, the only place noted in the McGoun book where food was sold was the Hey Grocery Store, which was purchased by Clifford Julian. It is, therefore, primarily a matter of conjecture as to exactly when any particular hotel, motel, trailer park, restaurant or club first opened its doors. Hence, in this chapter, the author asks for the reader's indulgence as we base those conjectures regarding any given or particular time period on the appearance not only of the facility itself but also of the surrounding area. For example, it can be noted that in one of the Old Heidelberg images, the restaurant appears to be standing almost completely alone, with perhaps one building visible in the background.

Because of the educated guesswork involved in determining approximate time periods, the reader should be able to ascertain the era or decade in which a particular building or facility existed and operated, and in several cases, the menus are also excellent clues. However, that being noted, it may be recalled that in Chapter 4 a restaurant in the northwest section was mentioned in regard to an untoward event that occurred on April 28, 1928. Although the restaurant was not named, it was located in the area now known as "the Palms," and it is entirely possible that, due to the segregation of the era, there may have been one or more restaurants in the northwest section of the town with no eating houses to the east for several years to come, a supposition that, given the still mostly rural character of Hallandale at the time, is both reasonable and logical.

Due to the dearth of documentable material or information on hospitality venue chronology, it is absolutely legitimate to make the most valid assumption that the very first hospitality-related businesses, other than the one or more restaurants in the northwest section noted in the paragraph immediately above, may very well have been the "tin can tourist camps," known within a few years later as "trailer courts" or "trailer parks."

Fortunately, there is photographic evidence of several being situated in the town, and thanks to the recollections of Hallandale Beach's vice-mayor, Bill Julian, we learn that "Hallandale was full of trailer parks...there were probably more people living in the [trailer] parks from the 1950s through the 1960s than in homes, because there were no condos then." The vice-mayor also related that "at that time all of the residents' homes were on the west side of town." Given the fact that this information was provided by what is known as a "primary source" (one who has been there and seen and done that), it would be difficult to argue or disagree with the conclusion that Mr. Julian has shared.

The lack of concrete and documentable information was not limited to McGoun's book, for the Thursday, May 5, 1977 issue of the *Hallandale Digest*, the predecessor of today's *South Florida Sun Times*, which was the paper's fiftieth anniversary commemorative issue and was dedicated to the city's history, contained, on page B12, an article about Manero's Restaurant, a longtime local favorite located on Hallandale Beach Boulevard adjacent to the Intracoastal Waterway bridge. However, with the exception of that article and mentions of John V. Nipes General Store and Farm Supplies, Hedrick's General Store and Farm Supplies (just south of Barnett's on Southeast First Avenue) and Seymour's Food Mart, there is no other mention of any place where it was likely that food for consumption on or off premises could be purchased, making this chapter a complete breakthrough in detailing the history of Hallandale Beach.

Given the lack of documentable evidence, it appears safe to conjecture that the first hospitality operations in the city were Tower Trailer Park (with the phone number "Hollywood 9208"), Seville Courts ("World's finest cottage and trailer park") and Homestead Cottage and Trailer Park, which featured "Private Tile Showers." The first inns, then, were either "cabins," "cottages" or "motor courts," and in all cases the visitor could bring his or her car to the front door and enjoy small, air-cooled (no air conditioning; open the window or turn on the fan!) rooms, which were very acceptable from late fall to early spring but must have been brutally hot in the summer. By the 1950s, motels such as the Dakar, the Sea Banks, the Flamingo, the Holiday Beach and the Gates Riviera opened on Ocean Drive (A1A), while other motels, including the Fredola, Badger Motor Court and Hodgson's Motor Court at 109 South Federal Highway, had opened on the mainland side.

Restaurants and nightclubs or lounges (other than the casinos) included Manero's, Driftwood Lounge, Hofbrau Haus, Old Heidelberg and the later ventures, including South Pacific, Sage Bagels and Deli, Nick's, Lum's (currently the twenty-four-hour Flashback Diner), Carini's, Doria's, Pumpernik's, the food and beverage outlets at Mardi Gras Racing and Casino (formerly Hollywood Dog Track), Gulfstream Racing and Casino and the numerous fast-food outlets on Federal Highway and Hallandale Beach Boulevard. Suffice to say, dining opportunities in Hallandale Beach today are virtually unlimited, ranging from the aforementioned restaurants to coffee shops, fine dining and everything in between, including a wide range of ethnic foods led by, but not limited to, Chinese and Thai, with sports bars, buffets and casual eateries thrown in for good measure.

Hallandale Beach today, with its Hampton Inn, oceanfront motels, wide range of dining opportunities, a casino at each of the two racetracks and the newly opened restaurants, bars and lounges at Gulfstream Village, has become a South Florida mecca for great times, great fun, great food and wonderful socializing, and the only thing that can be projected for Broward County's city of choice is a good bit more of the same!

Possibly Hallandale's oldest business catering to tourists, the Tower Trailer Park advertised that travelers could easily find it if they would "take right fork just south of Hallandale stop light." That right fork, of course, is today's Old Federal Highway, which begins just north of Flashback Diner, the obvious intimation being that, at the time, there was only one "stop light" in Hallandale, that being at the intersection of two-laned Hallandale Beach Boulevard and the four-lane Federal Highway (U.S. 1).

Because so many of the records have been lost or discarded through the years, there is no way today to ascertain the exact dates of the openings of the trailer parks, motor courts, cottages or cabins; hence, it is possible that the Seville Courts, "One Mile South [of] Hollywood, Florida," might have been a predecessor of the Tower Trailer Park. Interestingly, there is a sign on the front of the building at far left facing Federal Highway that reads "Kentucky Tavern." A close examination of the image shows people in front of and behind what appears to be a take-away counter. Guests were apparently able to enjoy their victuals under the umbrellas arrayed in front and on the side of what must be the reception building.

HOMESTEAD COTTAGES on Hwy No. 1 - 1 Mile So. of Hollywood Circle

Another of the earliest beacons for the tired traveler was the Homestead Cottage & Trailer Park, which, as shown on the sign, offered CBS (concrete block structure) construction, all-electric kitchens and tile baths. Opening date? A Hallandale Beach mystery that may never be solved.

One of the first of Hallandale's oceanfront motels was the Flamingo, which issued this attractive brochure featuring an artist's rendering of the building on the cover.

Along with the Flamingo, the Holiday Beach was one of the first oceanfront resorts. However, because Hallandale, at the time, was not the name that it is today and was basically unknown outside of the immediate area, the brochure shows the location as "Hollywood, Florida" but does note that the location is "Hallandale Road and A1A."

The SunAqua (one word!) Motel and Studio Apartments was at 1945 South Ocean Drive and offered eighty rooms and efficiency apartments as well as a coffee shop and restaurant.

The Dakar featured an African theme (note the zebra in front by the sign), a cocktail lounge and coffee shop, noting that the motel was "directly on the romantic Atlantic Ocean."

The Sea Banks, at 2000 Ocean Drive, advertised as being "located in a secluded area just north of Miami Beach." However, like so many of the Miami Beach and Bal Harbour hotels and motels of the time, the Sea Banks also noted in its advertising that it catered to a "carefully selected clientele," which meant that those of the Jewish faith were not welcome as guests.

The address of the Gates Riviera was 2080 Ocean Boulevard, rather than Ocean Drive, and, like the Sea Banks, played on Miami Beach's national fame by claiming that it was "just north of Miami Beach."

Just to be sure that it was recognized for more than the two racetracks, Hallandale had no problem with having beautiful girls—known as "cheesecake"—photographed on its beaches.

Hodgson's Motor Court, at 109 South Federal Highway, featured duplex-type cottages.

The Fredola, at 900 South Federal Highway, was operated by Mr. and Mrs. F.I. Biller. It was directly across the street from the famous Leone's Restaurant and next to the Hofbrau Haus.

Sun n' Fun Motel and Apartments was at 308 Northeast Second Street and promoted itself as being "located in quiet residential area" and "walking distance of Gulfstream Park & Hollywood Dog Track." The latter, however, was quite a lengthy walk!

This page: Besides the Palms Club and Bill's Place in the Palms (northwest) section of the city, there were several great and famous eateries that opened in Hallandale beginning in the 1950s, including Old Heidelberg on North Federal Highway, next to Hollywood Dog Track. The restaurant and its Bavarian Orchestra featured accordions, singing waiters and yodelers, shown here.

This page: When the Hofbrau Haus opened on South Federal Highway, the original building's sign read simply "The Hofbrau Haus" and the telephone number was "9623," but with great food and wonderful service, the restaurant expanded, and, as one may note, the new sign on the front of the building modestly read "World Famous Hofbrau Haus."

This and next page: The Hofbrau Haus brought its theme to every part of the dining experience: the restaurant's matchbooks invited the guest to "thrill to dining pleasures" while the menu carried through the Bavarian theme.

The Hofbrauhaus
RESTAURANT
Hofbrauhau
U. S. Highway One
Hallandale, Florida
Telephone Hollywood WAbash 2-7223

Another of Hallandale's favored dining spots was Manero's on the south side of Hallandale Beach Boulevard just west of the Intracoastal Waterway bridge. *Courtesy Vice-mayor Bill Julian.*

A night view of Manero's features a Cadillac with the huge tail fins so popular on cars in the very late 1950s.

The Driftwood Lounge, at 270 North Federal Highway, proudly featured David Casson on "The World's Only Three Keyboard Hammond Organ."

There were at least four full-scale casino operations in Hallandale, including La Boheme in the former Zetterlund Home on the oceanfront, Hollywood Country Club, "Potatoes" Kaufman's Old Plantation and Meyer Lansky's Colonial Inn, shown here. *From* Town Topics, *May 1977, courtesy BCHC.*

P. Lazarou-Amanna, known as "Toula" to all her friends and guests, went to work at Lum's on South Federal Highway as a waitress. Learning from the less than excellent management how *not* to do things, she worked through several name changes, including Gulfstream Diner and Broadway Deli, before finally buying it and taking it over as the incredibly successful open twenty-four-hours-per-day Flashback Diner. In front of Lum's (breakfast special, $1.19!) with another server, Toula is on the right. *Courtesy Flashback Diner.*

Broadway Deli, the former Lum's and Gulfstream Diner, shortly before becoming Flashback Diner. *Courtesy Flashback Diner.*

This page: For "fressing," "schmoozing" and noshing, there's nothing like Sage Bagel and Deli at 800 East Hallandale Beach Boulevard, for some years presided over by the late Milton Fuerst and now managed to the same high standards by his wife, Iris, who seems to know most of the restaurant's guests by name! *Courtesy Iris and Zachary Fuerst.*

This and next page: After several years of "going downhill," Nick's Restaurant, one of Hallandale's longtime favorites, at 105 East Hallandale Beach Boulevard, was bought by a group dedicated to "bringing it back," and that, indeed, they have done, with new specials, terrific food and gracious service. One of the owners, beautiful and charming Jacqueline Ortiz, is shown here with general manager Ignacio Dominguez, who goes out of his way to make certain that every guest is warmly welcomed and enjoys his or her meal. *Courtesy Nick's Restaurant.*

Nick's Coffee Selection
Earl Grey
English Teatime
Broiled Salmon
Baked Macaroni & Cheese
Lettuce Tomato
(1) Piece Fried Fish
Side of Macaroni & Chee
Sliced Pork Pickles
Swiss mustard
Cuban Sandwich
BBQ Beef Sandwich
Fries & Slaw
(5) Chicken Wing's
Fries — 7.99

Chapter 6

Buildings, Businesses and Stores

Unlike the hospitality genre, wherein little is known about the names or dates of the very first of the hotels, restaurants or clubs other than the fact that, as early as 1928, there was at least one—and likely more—restaurant(s) operating in the northwest section of the town, the historical chronicles have been kinder to the researcher who is seeking information on the history of the buildings, businesses and stores that have been part of Hallandale Beach's history.

As is the case in many (if not most) of the towns and cities on the east coast of Florida, the Florida East Coast Railway was either the first business to operate in and through that particular place or it was instrumental in enabling the first businesses to begin operation, and in Hallandale that was exactly the situation. As was noted in Chapter 1, Matilda, Henry and August Gieges began operating the rooming house that had been built by the Model Land Company on Halland Avenue to provide quarters for settlers prior to them constructing their own homes, and it is likely that that 1897 building was the first commercial building in the new settlement, followed closely by Luther Halland's trading post. The Hedrick, Nipe and Hey general stores soon followed, and the people of Hallandale had a choice of businesses in which they could spend their hard-earned money to purchase the goods, products, implements, supplies and equipment that they needed to start or operate their businesses.

Churches, schools and houses would follow, along with the packinghouses, of which, eventually, there were fourteen, most situated adjacent to the FEC

Railway tracks in order to expedite unloading of supplies and loading of truck (produce) and fruit, the diversity of the latter, from pineapples to strawberries to citrus, nothing short of amazing.

As the twentieth century rolled on, and as more and more people slowly came to the town, there would, with the coming of the great "boom" of the 1920s, be some not inconsequential development. In 1921, for example, the *Hallandale Herald*, in its April 12 edition, carried ads for John B. Hart's Pioneer Store "In the Heart of Hallandale/Corner Dixie Highway and Beach Drive," the Clawson Brothers Hallandale Garage—which, according to the ad, was "Right on the Dixie Highway, Near Ocean Drive," which must have been an early alternate name for Hallandale Beach Boulevard—and George W. Hedrick's Department Store, which carried his last name and was located "Opposite Depot" approximately where Barnett's is now.

In the early years of the boom, Hallandale was not unmindful of what was occurring to the north and south of the community, and although J.W. Moffitt opened a real estate brokerage and, in partnership with the Atlantic Shores Company, did plan a development east of Federal Highway a few blocks north of Beach Boulevard, there were only a few Mediterranean Revival–style homes built, several of which remain standing. It is that small group of houses that make up, according to William R. Adams in his fine article "Historic Hallandale," which appeared in the Winter–Spring 1993 *Broward Legacy* magazine, "Hallandale's most concentrated architectural legacy of the Great Boom."

There would be at least two commercial buildings built in that architectural style in 1925: the Gieges Building (which has, through the years, been considerably altered) on the northwest corner of Dixie Highway and Beach Boulevard and H.C. "Heinie" Schwartz's building, which bore his name, at 420 South Dixie Highway.

Numerous homes would be built in the southwest section, including the Curci house and the Moffitt house, while the Zetterlund Estate, later the La Boheme Casino, was built on the oceanfront. By 1926, the northwest section was bustling, with houses, apartments and small commercial buildings being built, while on the east side of the tracks there were at least four real estate firms, two drugstores, a lumber supply house, a meat and grocery store, two garages or service stations, a laundry and several churches.

Eventually, in 1941, city hall, which had been located at 124 Northwest Ninth Street from the town's formation, was moved to 308 South Dixie Highway. The new building, which included police headquarters and adjoining jail, replaced the two-story school building that had been on that site for some years.

As has been previously noted, the dog track first opened on December 12, 1934, at the north end of town, while Gulfstream Race Track would open briefly in 1939 and then close until, in 1944, Exotic Gardens (florists) owner Jimmy Donn Sr. would take over the track, resume racing and, in concert with the dog track, provide Hallandale with a steady stream of revenue with which to help fund municipal projects and enterprises.

By the mid-1950s, Hallandale was stirring as if from a deep sleep, and longtime land owner and Hallandale resident H.B. "Pappy" Layne and the Curcie brothers began building the Golden Isles development, which was to be followed by high-rise construction on both the ocean and mainland sides. Culminating Hallandale's growth spurt would be the construction of the Diplomat Mall, the country club of the same name and the gigantic Three Islands Development. In 1965, the Hallandale Jewish Center opened with 10 members, and twenty-one years later, the membership stood at 1,250.

The never-ending activities of the Hallandale Beach Area Chamber of Commerce must also be recognized, particularly given the work that current Executive Director Patricia Genetti has done to make the chamber such an important part of not only the business community but of the city itself. Although an attempt was made to start a chamber in 1947, the genesis of the present chamber was on July 13, 1953, at a meeting called by Earle W. Peterson. Merging the defunct chamber with another merchant's organization, the new chamber, electing John S. Fenn as its first president, laid the groundwork for the growth of an organization that has been at or in the forefront of every positive initiative that Hallandale and Hallandale Beach have engaged in. Today, with over two hundred members, the chamber is recognized as one of the most positive forces in the history of the city.

Hallandale Beach is, simply put, an amazing city, offering every kind and type of business and service in every kind and type of building that can be imagined. From automotive services to architects, from furniture to food stores, from gardens to gadgets, from computers to condo buildings, from exterminators to education and from fast-food to fine dining, Hallandale Beach is the place to find it, enjoy it or buy it, for few other villages, towns or cities in Florida can offer the range of services, dining, houses of worship, banking, shopping and gaming that "the city of choice" does. Today, this incredible city is not only "the city of choice" for every possible style and range of living but also as the place to come to in order to have a choice—an incredible choice—of the widest variety of buildings, businesses and stores to shop in, eat in or live in that a person can possibly imagine.

One of the Hallandale Beach Chamber of Commerce's past presidents, the late Carol Owen, was president of Family Bank. *Courtesy Hallandale Beach Area Chamber of Commerce.*

The bulwark of support for increasing business in Hallandale Beach, the chamber regularly publishes updated booklets and brochures promoting the area and its businesses. This piece is a pluperfect example.

Another marvelous chamber piece promoting the city is this superb brochure, which notes that Hallandale Beach is "Where businesses come to thrive, Where entertainment is abundant and where location is optimal."

Joe Kessel, of Keller Williams Elite Properties, is a strong believer in the work and importance of the chamber. Joe served as its acting president in 2008 when the then-current president was reassigned, following which he served full time as president in 2009.

The name and history of Barnett's Hardware, the site, the building and the Barnett family, is nothing short of incredible. On the corner of Hallandale Beach Boulevard and Southeast First Avenue since the first building and predecessor business opened in the early 1900s, the location was a filling station, grocery store and farm trade store until Herman Barnett, shown here in 1969, purchased the building in 1954. *Courtesy Gail Barnett Kappes.*

Barnett's first truck was equipped for any job, from the ladders attached to the side and the roof to the brooms on the fenders and the bucket on the front bumper. *Courtesy Gail Barnett Kappes.*

In 1981, celebrating the store's twenty-seventh year, Herman and Roslyn Barnett pose in front of the float that was used in the Peppermint Stick parade. Sitting on the float is the Barnetts' grandson Philip Kappes and store employee Darryl, whose last name, unfortunately, is unknown. *Courtesy Gail Barnett Kappes.*

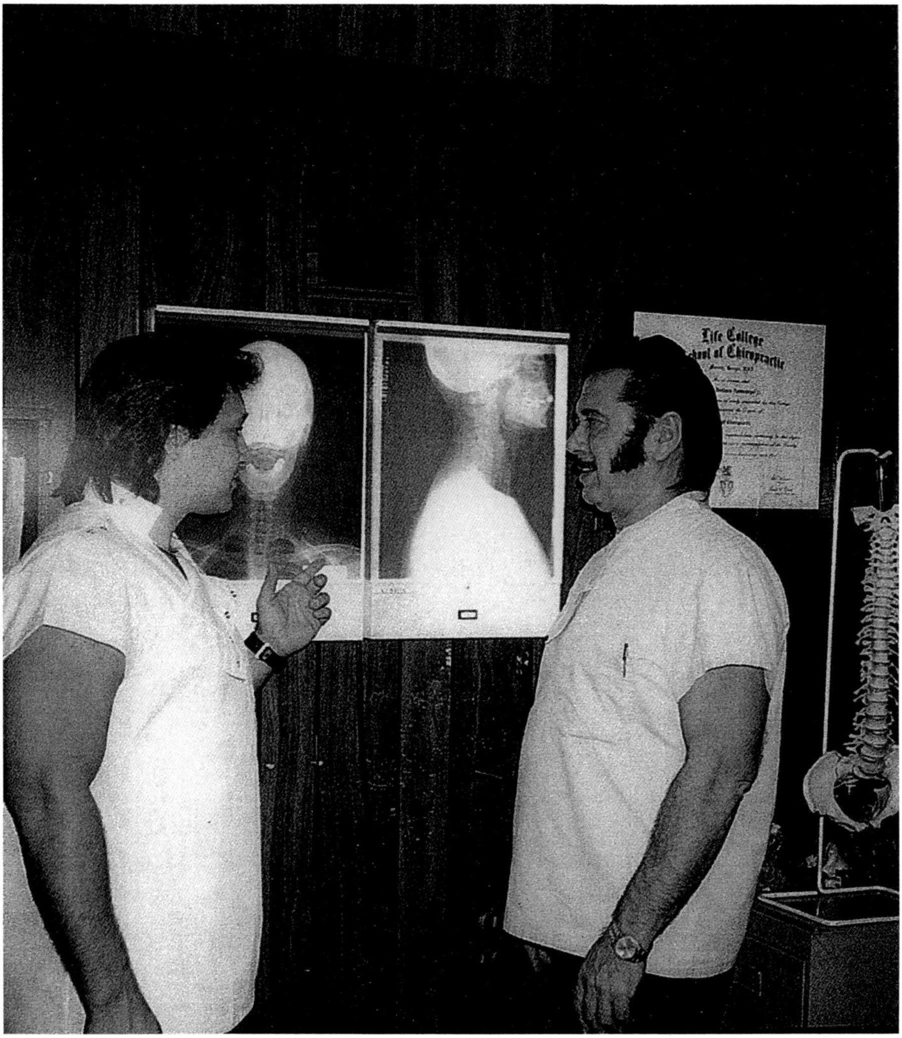

In 1973, Dr. Joseph A. Amunategui opened his chiropractic office in Hallandale. Today, son Joseph II, also a chiropractic physician, shown at left with his dad, serves his patients from his office at 1025 East Hallandale Beach Boulevard. The senior Dr. Amunategui was the first chiropractic physician in Hallandale Beach. *Courtesy Dr. J.A. Amunategui II.*

For some years, the post office was located on the site of today's Barnett's Hardware store and was eventually moved to a building on Southeast First Avenue, which is now used for administrative service. The new post office is on South Federal Highway. When the post office was on Southeast First Avenue, Arnold Lanner took this photo showing how uniquely Hallandale celebrates the holidays: Santa (Jim Wallace) is sharing not a candy cane but a miniature Danish with a delightedly pleased Marie Dowd. *CoHB.*

Longtime Hallandale resident Ellen Zimmerman worked at the Hallandale K-Mart for many years. In October 1997, supervisor LaVerne Smith presented Ellen with her five years of service pin. *Courtesy Ellen Zimmerman.*

Golden Isles Hospital was located just north of the entrance to Golden Isles. Because of the premium on space and the hospital's need to expand, the decision was made to move the operation to Hallandale Beach's neighboring city to the south, and today the healthcare institution is known as Aventura Hospital. *Courtesy Arthur Rosenberg.*

A major Hallandale Beach booster, Dave, of Tel Aviv Texaco at 126 North Federal Highway, has never hesitated to invest in his business or support his adopted city. Gas was somewhat lower priced when this photo, looking south on Federal Highway, was made. *Courtesy Tel Aviv Texaco.*

Offering a full line of automotive services, Dave features personalized car washes and detailing. The station, beautifully maintained, is shown here. *Courtesy Tel Aviv Texaco.*

Bernie Harrold has presided over Holiday Bowling Center, at 106 East Pembroke Road, for many years and never stops encouraging new and young bowlers. Shown here, having a great time at one of South Florida's few remaining bowling alleys (complete with restaurant, bar and billiard tables!) are, *from left*, John La'Torre, Celia Rocha, Michael McKenney and Ryan Nathan. *Courtesy Holiday Bowling Center.*

PAL of Hallandale Beach

Bowling Tournament

"Cops & Kids Together Filling Playgrounds, Not Prisons"

SPONSORED BY:

HBPD Community Involvement Unit ● PAL of Hallandale Beach ● Holiday Bowling Center

Sign your team up now to enter our 2010 Bowling Tournament.

Saturday, May 15, 2010 - 12:00pm
Holiday Bowling Center
106 Pembroke Road, Hallandale Beach
$80/per team of 4
(includes two games and bowling shoes)
Team Registrations ends on May 7, 2010

Registration begins at: 10:00am to 11:30pm

** Door Prizes **
** 50/50 Raffle **
** Free Commemorative T-Shirt for each participant **
** Individual trophies for top three teams **
** Trophy for highest score **
**Beat the Heat" Trophy if highest score beats Sgt. Beukers

To pre-register or provide donations/door prizes please contact:
Officer Christopher Taylor at 954-593-8010 or ctaylor@hallandalebeachfl.gov

Joining with the Hallandale Beach Police Department Community Involvement Unit and the PAL of Hallandale Beach, the bowling center hosted the 2010 team bowling tournament, the flyer shown here. Perhaps best of all? A "Beat the House" trophy if the highest score that day beat Sergeant Beukers's score! *Courtesy Holiday Bowling Center.*

Above: A view that will bring tears to no few eyes, as well as many warm and happy memories, is this photograph of two of Hallandale Beach's most beloved leisure-time businesses, Holiday Bowling Center on the right and the Hallandale Drive-In Theater at left. On the movie marquee? Two big thrillers: *The Curse of Frankenstein* and *X the Unknown*. Would that we could enjoy just one more show there, eh? *CoHB*.

Left: Hallandale Health Spa is one of the city's newest and most successful businesses, capitalizing on the area's renewed interest in nutritional awareness, physical fitness and skin care. In business since 1973, the environment, at 213 East Hallandale Beach Boulevard, is warm and welcoming.

Longtime Hallandale Beach businessman and general contractor Ed Pickett is shown with Patricia Kathy Conover, Hallandale's first female police department employee, at the 1999 Hallandale Historical Society holiday party. *Courtesy Ed Pickett.*

Keith Schuit, *back row, at left*, is vice-president of Community Bank of Broward at 929 East Hallandale Beach Boulevard. A "big-time" Hallandale Beach booster, Keith is active in the Rotary Club and the community. Standing next to him is Ramon Leyva, and in the front row are, *from left*, JoAnn Counihan, Barbara Gieske, Gloria Busse and security officer Bill Valdez. *Courtesy Keith Schuit.*

This page: For many years, Hallandale Beach's premier automobile dealer, Bill Kelley has continued the business that his dad began years ago in the same North Federal Highway location. Bill—in one of his great selling poses—and his Chevrolet dealership logo are pictured here. *Courtesy Bill Kelley.*

Bill
kelley
CHEVROLET
Hallandale Beach, Fla

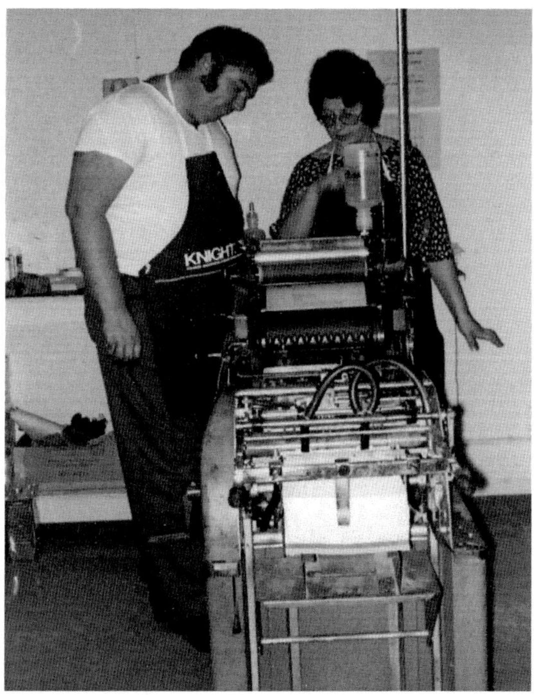

This page: Shown here in 1972 operating their printing presses are Susan and the late Michael Mandel. Now operating Hallandale Creative Printing at 306 West Hallandale Beach Boulevard, Susan, an active Rotary Club member, is Hallandale Beach's foremost printer and has been in business longer than any other print shop in the city. *Courtesy Susan Mandel.*

This and next page: Hallandale's oldest school, originally at West Beach Boulevard and Second (or Third) Avenue (McGoun and the *Hallandale Digest* give two different addresses), was moved to Northwest Seventh Avenue, where it became the Hallandale Beach Police Department's D.W. (Bill) Baxter PAL Building. Through the CRA and a $50,000 grant from County Commissioner Sue Gunzburger's discretionary fund, over $224,000 has been raised to restore the school, which will be partly original schoolhouse and partly a museum. Juxtapositioned with that edifice in terms of age is Hallandale Beach High School, which opened in 1975 in temporary quarters in the old Lanier Middle School building. *BCHC; high school photo by Ed Halland.*

HALLANDALE HIGH SCHOOL

An absolutely incredible photograph, taken by Hollywood *Sun-Tattler* photographer James M. Urick in 1983, shows the famous Ocean Drive and Hallandale Beach Boulevard landmark water tower being painted by one fearless guy! *BCHC.*

For the December 18, 1974 Peppermint Stick parade, the Rotary Club's Mrs. Robert Greaver joined Santa's reindeer on the club's float and was warmly applauded as she waved to the onlookers. Sun-Tattler *photo by John Ashcraft Jr., courtesy BCHC.*

Chapter 7
Mardi Gras Casino and Hollywood Dog Track

December 12, 1934, was a bitter cold night in South Florida when Bill Syms, having invested $50,000 on a plot of land on the south side of Pembroke Road fronting on the west side of Federal Highway, gambled on Hallandale as the right place for the right business at the right time. At the appointed moment, he gave his employees the signal to open the gates to the new and newly named Hollywood Dog Track, and as cold as it was, more than twelve thousand hardy racing fans surged through the gates, wagering more than $12,000 on the dogs, and that, for the time and as the saying goes, "waren't hay!" But to really understand what "bitter cold" meant and how impressive the twin twelve thousand numbers are, it was possibly the coldest December 12 ever recorded in Hollywood and Hallandale, the temperature that night reaching a low of thirty degrees Fahrenheit.

In the height of the Depression, even with the Art Deco boom beginning on Miami Beach and the terrible Labor Day 1935 hurricane—which turned over an FEC train on Matecumbe Key, destroyed forty miles of track and caused the abandonment of the Key West Extension less than nine months in the future—the opening of the track was of such consequence that numerous celebrities attended. When, in the first race, Buddy Hawke upset the favored Ben Andrews and paid sixty-two dollars to win, the trophy was presented to Buddy's owner by none other than Mrs. Damon Runyon, wife of the famous columnist.

In 1940, a clubhouse was added to the track, which, up until that time had only grandstand seating, and in 1953 an annex to the grandstand was built. In 1961, the grandstand facing the far turn was added, and the administration building was enlarged shortly thereafter. At some point in time—prior to the 1947 season—the Hollywood Dog Track became the Hollywood Kennel Club, the name it retained until the advent of re-legalized (through an amendment to the Florida constitution) gaming in the form of cards and slot machines in 2004.

In 1964, the track was purchased by Castleton Industries, which also owned the Pompano Harness Track, and by 1974 the capacity of the facility stood at twenty-five thousand, with space for 3,600 cars. A matinee or evening's entertainment included luncheon or dinner, people watching and, of course, betting on one's favorite canine racer.

Unfortunately, as was the case with the parimutuels industry throughout the country, the effects of legalized casino gaming in places such as Nevada, Atlantic County, New Jersey, and the Caribbean were beginning to take a toll, and slowly but inexorably the crowds shrank and the "handle" (the amount of money wagered) dropped precipitously. Throughout Florida, a good few horse and dog tracks and jai alai frontons—which were specifically exempted from the ban on "games of chance" when the state constitution was rewritten in 1938, outlawing what had, for two years, been completely legal—went into decline, some meeting the wrecking ball as they were closed due to declining revenues.

In Dade County alone, although Calder Race Course opened, Tropical Park closed, as did Miami Beach and Biscayne Kennel Clubs. Only through constant advertising and unending promotions, as well as leasing parking lot space on weekends for "flea markets," were the remaining dog and horse tracks and the jai alai frontons able to survive.

As it became more evident and obvious that a major industry and a major employer and generator of tax revenue for the host cities and counties as well as the entire state was in jeopardy, several attempts were made to legalize casinos through constitution-amending referendums. But most of them were poorly organized and completely uncoordinated, with perhaps the sloppiest of all and the one that met with the most derision and the largest losing vote the attempt to specifically name areas of Miami Beach, along with all of the state's parimutuels, as venues for the casinos. Fortunately for the parimutuel and the gaming industries, as well as the state, cooler heads, better financed and more organized, would eventually carry the day.

In 2004, a statewide vote to amend the constitution to allow slot machines only in parimutuels and only in Miami-Dade and Broward Counties was passed by the electorate, with the caveat that each of the two counties would have to have a second vote to approve the proposal. On Tuesday, March 8, 2005, Broward County's voters approved the referendum, and the state legislature then passed the enabling act, which allowed the slot machines to be placed in the parimutuels. The amendment, incidentally, required the continuation of either racing or jai alai at any of the facilities that chose to install slot machines.

On December 26, 2006, following final approval by the legislature, a major and massive renovation, building of new dining rooms, snack bars and cocktail lounges and the installation of 1,300 slot machines, a magnificent new facility opened to huge crowds and rave reviews.

When the casino opened, the name was changed from Hollywood Greyhound Track to Mardi Gras Gaming and Race Track Center, but over the last several years the name was upgraded to Mardi Gras Casino, and that is the name that is being used on all of the casino/track's advertising and promotional branding material.

Under the astute management of Vice-president Dan Adkins, revenues continue to increase, and among the major draws, besides the opportunity to "hit it big" in the card rooms, on the slots or with one of the never-ending and always exciting promotional events, is the fact that Mardi Gras Casino prohibits smoking, thus encouraging large numbers of additional patrons.

With a casino and parimutuel at each end of the city, Hallandale Beach is one of the few cities in Florida, especially of its size, to boast gaming in two locations. At Mardi Gras, the games of chance are enhanced by the beautiful and beautifully outfitted gracious and cordial young women who welcome every visitor. With live racing, simulcasting, great slots and so much to do, Mardi Gras Casino brings 'em back time after time for fun and games, wonderful food and drink and a wholesome and safe environment. Suffice to say, Mardi Gras, as it does in New Orleans, means great crowds, great entertainment and great fun!

Left: The Thursday, March 20, 1947 racing program features an attractive woman walking an anxious greyhound to the starting gate. The tag line on the program states that Hollywood Kennel Club was presenting "the aristocracy of racing greyhounds."

Below: This incredible circa 1938–39 image, courtesy of Vice-mayor Bill Julian, shows a much different dog track—and city—than exists today. The grandstand backs up to Federal Highway, which is a narrow four lanes. Pembroke Road is the street at far right, and the base of the "Dog Track" sign at lower right actually appears to be extending into the northbound highway lanes.

Right: For several years, to bring people in more quickly from the huge parking lots, the track instituted tram service with Hawaiian-theme outfitted women as hostesses. *Courtesy Mardi Gras Casino.*

Below: To help celebrate the city of Hallandale's fiftieth anniversary, the track's final day of the 1977 racing season—May 21—the kennel club hosted the event, the huge Federal Highway bulletin board ballyhooing the gala function. *CoHB.*

This and next page: A track employee shows one of the celebrity greyhounds his picture in one of the programs while the track announcer gives results to the large crowd during the heyday of racing. *Courtesy Mardi Gras Casino.*

Griese goes to the dogs

Miami Dolphin quarterback Bob Griese relaxes at the Hollywood Greyhound Track with his wife Judi. It was Bob's first visit to Hollywood's new facility now in its third year of operation. And his reaction to the palace of greyhound racing was "It's fantastic."

Shula's a winner

Miami Dolphin Head Football Coach Don Shula managed to take time out from his pressing off-season business to enjoy an evening at the Hollywood Greyhound Track in Hallandale. Joining Shula was veteran WCKT-TV sportscaster George Mills. It was Shula's first visit to Hollywood and it proved beneficial as he hit the first race quiniela for $75.

This page: Shown enjoying the races in 1973 are Miami Dolphins Super Bowl seasons quarterback Bob Griese, his wife Judy and Dolphins coach Don Shula with Miami's Channel Seven sportscaster George Mills. It was both Griese's and Shula's first of many visits to the track. *Courtesy Mardi Gras Casino.*

This page: The Mardi Gras era began with a bang as one of the ladies, in full costume, introduces the new look to one of the greyhounds while two of the athletically inclined women, dressed as harlequins, perform for the crowd. *Courtesy Mardi Gras Casino.*

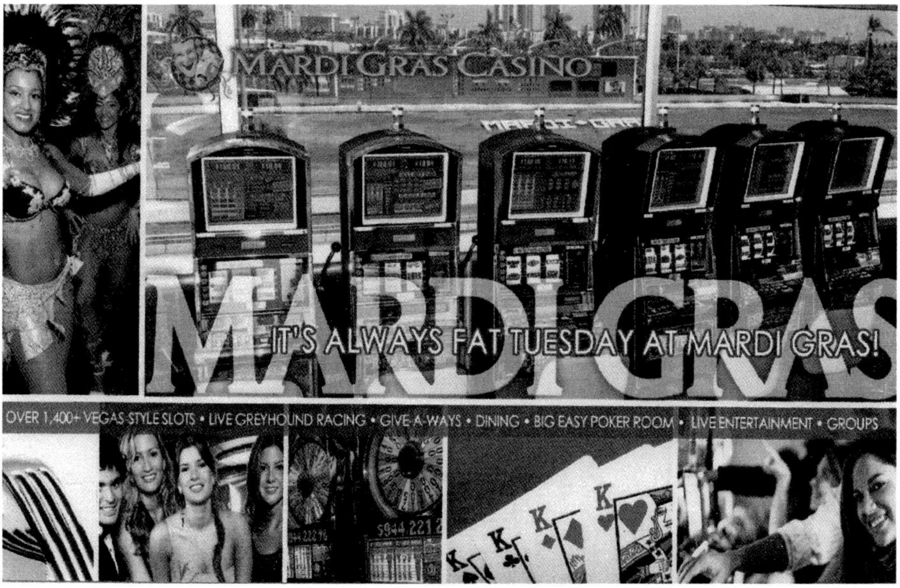

One of the casino's advertising cards, replete with smiling and happy faces, lets the reader know that "It's Always Fat Tuesday at Mardi Gras!" *Courtesy Mardi Gras Casino.*

Poker and blackjack are big draws at Mardi Gras, and the Big Easy Poker Room invites players to "show us your poker face." *Courtesy Mardi Gras Casino.*

Above: An inviting atmosphere, complete with Mardi Gras decorations, beckons the slot players. *Courtesy Mardi Gras Casino.*

Right: It's not just gaming or racing that attracts visitors to Mardi Gras. The dining opportunities—the Crab Leg Shrimp Fest promotional shown here—are numerous and diverse. *Courtesy Mardi Gras Casino.*

This page: It's not just "slots gone wild" at Mardi Gras that "brings 'em in" but, in addition, the stunningly beautiful young women who make every visitor feel comfortable and welcome keep the casino's guests coming back time after time. *Courtesy Mardi Gras Casino.*

Chapter 8
Gulfstream Park and Casino

It is said that "thoroughbred racing is the sport of kings," and if that longtime homily has any truth at all to it then the Donn family—James, James Jr. and Doug—were, for the fifty years that they owned Gulfstream Park Race Track, the kings of the sport.

The story of Gulfstream and of how James Donn Sr., at the time the owner of the famous Greater Miami floral and landscaping company the Exotic Gardens, took control of the track almost five years after its first owner made some terrible managerial miscalculations and then left a string of unpaid bills has become almost legendary, not only in horse racing circles but in the greater South Florida community, for it combines the best elements of a good few stories, fables and fairy tales. But in this one, "the good guys" really do come out as, happily for the racing industry, the city of Hallandale and all of South Florida, "the winners."

The history of Gulfstream began on Wednesday, February 1, 1939, when Jack Horning opened the track for horse racing five years after the dog track had opened. Incredibly, on opening day, the employees were unable to control the huge crowd of between fifteen and eighteen thousand people (depending on which source one wishes to accept as correct, but, and in any case, an immense mass of humanity!), which crashed through gates, broke down fences and barriers and generally created no small amount of havoc.

The handle that day, a little more than four years after the dog track opened with twelve thousand people present and a handle of $12,000, was

$224,287, not in any way, shape or form a "dig" at the dog track's play on its opening day but, rather, to the historian, an indication that a nation was finally emerging from the worst Depression in its history and that the people who came to enjoy the track that day had money and were willing to spend it.

Famed ice skater Sonja Henie was in the crowd on opening day, but that was the pinnacle of the first year's operation, for that "season," if it can be called that, lasted a grand total of four days, the handle for that meet totaling $441,561. And why did racing end after only four days? Simply put, because Horning made two huge mistakes: he did not have sufficient cash on hand to meet his obligations, including the money required for the betting windows, and, perhaps even worse, he foolishly chose to open, in an era before racing dates were regulated by the state, at the height of Hialeah's racing season. For Miami-area tourists, Gulfstream was in the wilderness and was too far away from Miami and Miami Beach hotels. One of the most common comments was, "Who wants to go way up there into the middle of nowhere when we can take an FEC special train direct to Hialeah?"

The famous Hialeah Park, long established, and considered even then America's most beautiful thoroughbred track, was simply too much of a draw for Gulfstream to compete against. Unhappily, following the fourth day of racing, Horning, dejected and completely out of cash, closed the track, which would not reopen again until 1944 and then not in competition with Hialeah.

During the five-year racing interim, the American military found it quite convenient to avail itself of what, even then, was a major piece of somewhat improved property and, as with so much else of South Florida during World War II, took possession of the track in 1940. They used the facility for storage of materiel and armaments as well as for training operations for ground troops until 1943, when they moved operations from Hallandale to other nearby facilities, particularly close-by naval air stations at Miami, Opa Locka and Fort Lauderdale, leaving the property ready for the segue into private hands.

In 1944, James Donn Sr., who, as noted, owned the Exotic Gardens and was one of the park's major creditors, stepped in to reestablish the track as a horse racing venue. Gulfstream, coming back to life that first year, ran a twenty-day race meeting, and while none of the new owners got rich, the meet was successful: attendance for the twenty days averaged 4,534, with a handle that averaged $281,902, which, given wartime conditions, gas, oil, tire and rubber rationing, road conditions and a park that was still considered to be "out in the boonies," was certainly respectable.

The following season, the track ran its first regular meeting of forty days with average attendance more than doubling to 10,699 and average handle increasing by close to two and a half times to $714,801.

In 1947, with Gulfstream now a fixture on the South Florida parimutuels scene, Hallandale, in becoming a city and expanding its boundaries west of U.S. 1 for the first time, annexed the track's property into the new city. Since then, Gulfstream has been able to boast proudly that it is located in then Hallandale and now Hallandale Beach, Florida.

By 1952, with business increasing steadily, the first clubhouse was erected, an addition to the grandstand was built and the Florida Derby, won by Sky Ship, was run at Gulfstream for the first time. In 1964, James Donn Jr., son of the legendary founder, became Gulfstream's president, following which he oversaw the installation of what was, at the time, the largest tote board in the world, which was erected in the track's infield.

James Donn Jr. was always open to new ideas and new thoughts as to how to increase revenue, and in May 1968, according to Hallandale Beach's vice-mayor, Bill Julian, the first real outdoor rock concert in the United States was held at Gulfstream Park. It was produced on a minimal budget by the same three men who would go on to produce another outdoor rock concert in New York State, called (even though it wasn't actually held there) "Woodstock," but Gulfstream park was where they "cut their eye teeth."

An interesting sidelight to the Gulfstream concert is that Debbie Smith, a current Hallandale Beach resident, designed all of the psychedelic posters for the event, which featured, among others, Jimi Hendrix, Steppenwolf, The Who and other groups that would go on to international fame through Woodstock. Current Hallandale Beach commissioner and former mayor Dorothy Ross was a member of the Hallandale Police Department when the concert was held, and Vice-mayor Julian was in the crowd, he having paid the grand sum of six dollars for his ticket!

Upon Mr. Donn's passing, in 1978, his son, Doug Donn, was elected Gulfstream Park president, a title that he retained until the sale of the track to Bertram and Diane Firestone, owners of Miami's Calder Race Course, in 1990. However, prior to selling the track, Doug arranged for Gulfstream to host, in 1989, the fabled Breeders Cup World Championships, breaking almost every attendance and handle record in Florida history. With that triumph, the stage was set for the sale.

On December 27, 1991, the Firestones sold the park through a company called Catoctin International to Gulfstream Holdings, Inc., a subsidiary of Orient Corporation, a Japanese-owned firm, which, in September

1999 sold the track to Magna Entertainment Corporation (MEC). In 2004, Magna began work on a massive project to create a whole new entertainment and shopping village at the track, which would coincide perfectly with the initiation of casino operations in November 2006. On January 3, 2007, thoroughbred racing and slot machines were in perfect sync as, for the first time in Florida history, legalized casino gaming and horse racing operated simultaneously.

With the first phase of the Village at Gulfstream Park opening in early 2010 as a development of MEC and real estate developer Forest City Enterprise, the Village's next step will be to build the first mixed-use retail and lifestyle center anchored by a racetrack in America, while future phases will include residential and office space as well as a hotel, thereby permitting guests to enjoy Gulfstream Park and Casino as a complete package destination, something that, before the legalization of casino gaming, would not have been possible. Suffice to say, Gulfstream's future will be nothing short of spectacular!

While Jimmy Donn Sr. did not build the original Gulfstream Park, it was he who brought it to the pinnacle of horse racing following the acquisition of the track in 1944 by the group that he headed. *Courtesy Gulfstream Park and Casino.*

Jimmy Donn Jr. took over management of the track and park in 1964 and remained chairman until his passing in 1978, at which time he was succeeded by his son, Doug. *Courtesy Gulfstream Park and Casino.*

A circa 1960 aerial view shows the clubhouse from above. All of the parking lots in front of the clubhouse are now part of Gulfstream Village, the parking area now to the south and north of the track. *Courtesy Gulfstream Park and Casino.*

We can date this marvelous image to circa 1958, as we look northeast toward the beach and the now long-gone Gulfstream drive-in theatre on East Hallandale Beach Boulevard. Golden Isles had been filled, but Beach Boulevard was essentially empty, a condition that would not last more than another year or two. *CoHB.*

In 1978, Doug Donn, handsome, dapper, youthful and gracious, took over management of the track and, during his tenure as president, expanded Gulfstream's facilities. In 1989, he arranged for the track to host the first ever Breeder's Cup World Championships to be held in Florida. Doug, shown here with his beautiful wife, Alice, was honorary chairman of the Breeder's Cup Ball. *CoHB*.

Doug, with his mother, Gulfstream's vice-chairman of the board, Mary Anna Fowler, shortly before the sale of the track to the Firestones. *CoHB*.

This page: Florida Derby was the highlight of the Gulfstream season, capped by the race, a gala ball and the selection of the Derby Queen. In 1964, the selection committee chose twin co-queens, Karlene and Darlene Sanks, and in 1977, stunningly beautiful Mary Alice Wilson was named queen. *CoHB.*

George Julian was a thoroughbred owner and trainer for almost his entire life, and from 1955 to 1998 he raced at Gulfstream as well as Tropical Park, Hialeah and Calder racecourses. Julian, shown here in 1966 with champion stakes winner Inclusive, imbued his son, William, with the same love of racing—and of Hallandale—that he had. *Courtesy Vice-mayor Bill Julian.*

The 1966 Florida Derby luncheon program featured Ruth Galvin as mistress of ceremonies and the crowning of that year's Derby Queen. *CoHB.*

Deborah and Joe Namath with famed thoroughbred Country Road. "Broadway Joe" served as spokesman for the track's 1985 advertising campaign, the season that year opening on January 8. *CoHB.*

In 1990, famed jockey Willie Shoemaker (shown here with James Donn Jr.) rode Beau Genius to the last victory of his incredible career. *Courtesy Doug Donn.*

On November 6, 2006, for the first time since being outlawed by constitution in 1938, slots were once again legal. A massive crowd waited anxiously as Gulfstream Race Track and Casino became the first parimutuel operation in Florida to initiate slots and poker, and on January 3, legalized slots and horse racing operated simultaneously at Gulfstream, another first in Florida history. *Courtesy Gulfstream Park Racing and Casino.*

The immense draw of the numerous entertainment and dining venues at the Village at Gulfstream Park brought the Aventura–Sunny Isles Beach Chamber to Texas de Brasil on February 2, 2010. Shown here, *from left*, are chamber director Les Winston, director Paul Klein, president David Sheinheit, marketing director Jon Rogoff, Hallandale Beach mayor Joy Cooper, public relations director Sid Gersh, chamber founder and president emeritus Emil Huebschman, member Joan Balkin and Sunny Isles Beach vice-mayor Lou Thaler. *Courtesy Joel Black.*

This page: In two photographs especially prepared by Gulfstream for this book, the slot machines in the casino beckon the players day and night while the poker and blackjack tables are always crowded with card-playing aficionados. *Courtesy Gulfstream Park Racing and Casino.*

Ken Dunn is Gulfstream's highly respected president and general manager. *Courtesy Gulfstream Park Racing and Casino.*

Frank Stronach, Gulfstream Park Racing and Casino's chairman of the board. *Courtesy Gulfstream Park Racing and Casino.*

Chapter 9
Great People, Great Diversity

In 1900, as the astute reader will recall from the first chapter, there were twelve families living in the area that would someday be formally named Hallandale, and two of the twelve were black. In essence, even though temporarily but unhappily interrupted by the terrible social evil of segregation, the black community was an integral part of Hallandale's history from, literally, the first day.

In fact, it should be noted that due to segregation, it appears that the northwest section of Hallandale, the area today known as the Palms, is now able to boast that it had restaurants, retail stores of various kinds and, possibly, even nightclubs before there were any such diversions east of Dixie Highway or south of Hallandale Beach Boulevard. Interestingly though, in the earliest years, blacks and whites worked together as farmers, in the packinghouses and as employees of the Florida East Coast Railway, both at the Hallandale depot and on the section gangs that maintained the track and right of way.

Beginning in the early 1930s, a number of Bahamians came to Hallandale to work and became strongly involved in the community. Among the names from this group that must be memorialized are the Ingram, Rolle, Pratt, Dean, Smith, Bain and John Cooper families.

Perhaps best of all, many Hallandallians warmly remember that going to nightclubs in what used to be known as "the northwest section" was not only safe but that a good few white youth were regulars to and welcomed at clubs such as the Palms. Eddie Pickett fondly remembered some gloriously grand times there, reveling in the music of no few of the great black rock and rollers including, among others, Aretha Franklin.

Unquestionably, during the days of segregation no few black residents worked and fought for an end to that peculiar institution but never to the point or level of violence, and there was always, in Hallandale, a desire to work peacefully together to achieve the goals of fairness and equality. Today, a good many Hallandale residents are proud of their beliefs in those principles and the fact that while other cities and areas of the South were blighted with the blood of unspeakable acts, the people of Hallandale—all of the people—generally understood that justice for all was the goal, and understanding that allowed them, for the most part, to work together to achieve that goal, in many cases long before most other places in the South were able to do so.

Hallandale has been blessed by having businesspeople, civic activists, artists, teachers and politicians in the black community who worked for the good of the entire community and, in many cases, may have understood even better than some in the white community did that fairness and equality must be the province of all, not just those with light-colored skin.

Among the many who worked so hard in the past to help build the city were the late Virdreatha Reynolds Eaton; the late Jonny Lee James, whose nursery supplied plants and other flora to much of Hallandale; and the late pioneer O.B. Johnson. Today, Hallandale is fortunate to have as an active part of the community people such as former army special services veteran and longtime local photographer Willie Washington; well-known grant writer and director of human resources of the Hepburn Center Mary Washington; Moreen Ware of Sonny's Restaurant; Hallandale High coach Greg Samuels; Reverend Joseph Johnson of Ebenezer Baptist Church; and Reta Mills, who owns a tax preparation firm and formerly managed the James Nursery.

John Saunders was the city's first black commissioner, while currently serving on the commission is Anthony Sanders. Among those who work daily on behalf of and promoting the city they love and call home are John Hardwick, Virginia Kilpatrick, Emerson Hawkins (longtime owner of Hawkins Bar-B-Q) and Qunea Gordon, founder and chairlady of the Hallandale High School Alumni Association.

Among the black community's many civic activists are Ida May Gilbert, Pearla May Thompson, Dorothy Barnes, Margaret Adams and Mrs. Olga Cooper.

In 2003, through the input of area residents, the name "the Palms" was voted on by northwest Hallandale residents as the official name for that area of the city. Much of the credit for that choice, partly commemorating the famous nightclub of the same name, went to the incredibly hard work of committee chairwoman Mary Washington, the committee members and John Hardwick. Northwest Eighth Avenue, which is Martin Luther King Jr. Boulevard, originally went from Hallandale Beach Boulevard north to Pembroke Road, but through the efforts of Vice-mayor Bill Julian, the MLK name was extended from Beach Boulevard south to the Dade-Broward County line.

The Palms now extends from I-95 on the west to Dixie Highway on the east and from Hallandale Beach Boulevard on the south to Pembroke Road on the north. The civic spirit in the area is incredible, and from all indications the Palms is preparing to embark on a major renaissance, with new businesses opening and investors such as Eagle's Wings Development Center putting their faith in the neighborhood. Indeed, as John Hardwick likes to say, "My business is here, my life is here, my friends are here and my future is here and all of that depends on all of us working together to build an ever greater Hallandale Beach!"

With people such as Commissioner Anthony Sanders, Mary Washington, John Hardwick and so many others leading the way, the future for not just the Palms but all of Hallandale Beach cannot be anything but gloriously bright.

Homegoing Celebration For

Elijah Johnson

1929 -- 2001

Tuesday, July 31, 2001
11:00 A. M.

Ebenezer Missionary Baptist Church
816 N. W. 1st Avenue, Hallandale, Florida

Reverend Joe C. Johnson, Pastor/Officiating

E. A. Stevens Funeral Home, Directing

"There Is No Substitution For Experience"

While not the very first, the greatly admired and respected Elijah Johnson (1929–2001) was one of the city's first black police officers. *Courtesy Virginia Kilpatrick.*

The woman who many consider "the mother of the northwest community," Maudie Lee "Marty" James, moved to Hallandale permanently in 1962. Her wisdom and insights are sought out frequently by community leaders of all colors and persuasions. *Courtesy John Hardwick.*

The late Virdreatha Reynolds Eaton was one of the northwest community's most active, proactive and respected civic activists. *CoHB.*

The first location for Bill's Place, a wonderful snack and sundry shop, was at Northwest Fifth Street and Foster Road. Bill Williams himself is standing behind the counter in this marvelous 1950 photograph. *Courtesy the Williams family.*

The Snack Shop moved to 708 Foster Road and featured its famous in South Broward County "Super Ghetto Burger." Holding the sign are, *from left*, Venetta Williams and her dad and mom, Willie and Eva Williams. After the Williams family sold the store to John Hardwick, he operated Fresh Cuts Barber Shop there for almost eighteen years. Today, the location is the home of Metro Outernet.com, a digital marketing company that serves the South Florida community. *Courtesy the Williams family.*

Ahead of the curve as always, Hallandale's schools, public and parochial, moved quickly to integrate, and one year after the passing of the Civil Rights Act of 1964 became law, St. Matthew School had integrated smoothly and without problems. Seventh- and eighth-grade teacher Arthur R. Schrage is shown with his young charges, including Patty Anderson in the second row from left and Billy Washington in the second row from the right. *Courtesy Billy Anderson.*

Fresh Cuts Barber Shop held sway at 708 Foster Road for almost two decades and is now the location of Metro Outernet.com. *Courtesy John Hardwick.*

Sonny's Triangle Restaurant, at 888 Foster Road, is owned by Willie "Sonny" Wolf. *Courtesy "Sonny" Wolf.*

Shown here with his Hallandale High School Chargers basketball team, Coach Greg Samuels exemplifies the Hallandale Beach spirit. A longtime HBHS teacher and coach, Samuels, in 1987, led the Chargers to the Florida State high school basketball championship. *Courtesy John Hardwick.*

Hallandale High community liaison Olga Harris poses proudly with famed HHS graduate Tampa Bay Buccaneers #75, Dalvin Joseph. *Courtesy Virginia Kilpatrick.*

Chesta Bird, *seated front row center*, and Qunea Gordon, *second row center*, founded the Hallandale High School Alumni Association. *Courtesy Qunea Gordon.*

William H. Sands Jr. founded Sands Shoe Repair and is shown in his store in 1948. *Courtesy Virginia Kilpatrick and John Hardwick.*

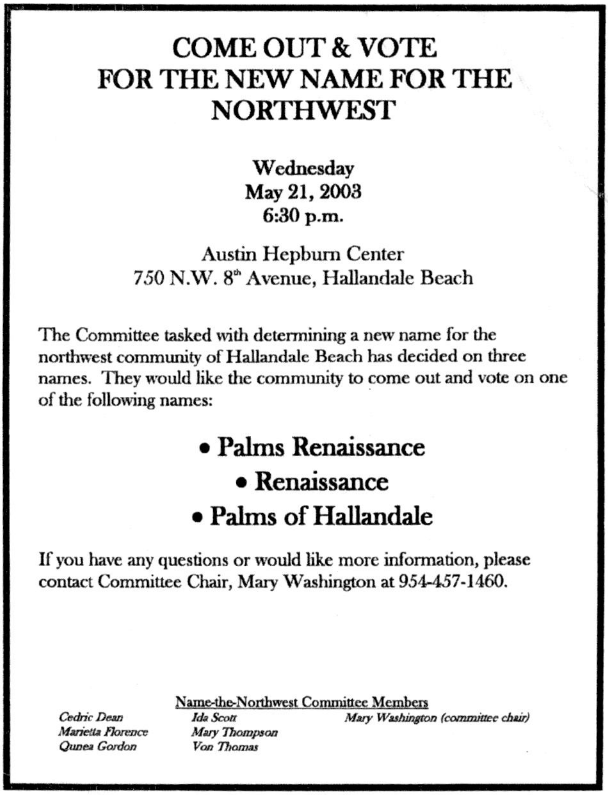

COME OUT & VOTE
FOR THE NEW NAME FOR THE
NORTHWEST

Wednesday
May 21, 2003
6:30 p.m.

Austin Hepburn Center
750 N.W. 8th Avenue, Hallandale Beach

The Committee tasked with determining a new name for the northwest community of Hallandale Beach has decided on three names. They would like the community to come out and vote on one of the following names:

- **Palms Renaissance**
- **Renaissance**
- **Palms of Hallandale**

If you have any questions or would like more information, please contact Committee Chair, Mary Washington at 954-457-1460.

Name-the-Northwest Committee Members

Cedric Dean *Ida Scott* *Mary Washington (committee chair)*
Marietta Florence *Mary Thompson*
Qunea Gordon *Von Thomas*

Left: On May 21, 2003, the northwest community voted for a new name for itself and selected "the Palms of Hallandale Beach," the very rare flyer promoting the election shown here. *Courtesy John Hardwick.*

Below: Having worked extraordinarily hard on behalf of the winning name, Hallandale Beach native John Hardwick takes a moment to have his photo taken in front of the new sign.

Chapter 10
Taking Hallandale Beach into the Future

There is something very special about Hallandale Beach. From the condos and motels along the oceanfront to Golden Isles, Three Islands, the business communities, the restaurants, the casinos and parimutuels and the Palms to the people, from Luther Halland and Olof Zetterlund to Frank Curci, J.W. Moffitt, Shirt Tail Charlie, the town's first mayor (Oliver White), the Gieges family, Heinie Schwartz, former mayor and current councilwoman Dorothy Ross, the city's first female mayor (Eudyce Steinberg), the police department's first female employee (Patricia Kathy Conover), Hallandale's first black commissioner (John Saunders), "Sonny" Ware, Virginia Kilpatrick, Mary Washington and current mayor Joy Cooper, Hallandale Beach was, is and will always be a very special place.

There were, to be sure, "fits and starts," but with the 1971 publication of a beautiful, glossy, color cover Hallandale promotional book by the chamber of commerce, the publication of Bill McGoun's book *Hallandale* in 1976 and the city's fiftieth anniversary celebration in 1977, replete with the *Hallandale Digest*'s fiftieth anniversary issue, the city began moving much more strongly and confidently into the future while, as the years have passed since, recognizing the importance of preserving its past.

The city's leadership has sometimes been progressive, sometimes quirky and sometimes quarrelsome but never, no matter who the person in the mayor's chair was, anything but filled with the best of intentions for the city's future.

After ten years of enjoying Hallandale as a "snowbird," Eudyce Steinberg and her husband "moved to Florida." In 1991, she was elected vice-mayor, becoming mayor in 1993, and it was she who initiated the move to build the city's community cultural center and the beautiful and modern city hall on South Federal Highway, which opened in 1997. Today, thirty years after moving permanently to Hallandale Beach, she still loves the city.

Before and after her (to name just a few) were mayors Aaron T. Canon, Milton Weinkle, Samuel B. Waterman, Arthur J. "Sonny" Rosenberg, Gilbert B. Stein, Dorothy Ross, Arnold N. Lanner, Joseph Scavo and Joy Cooper, all of whom have worked diligently in the service of the city.

Longtime city manager D. Mike Good has steered the city and supported business and the saving of the city's historic sites for many years, while people such as Police Chief Thomas A. Magill and Fire Chief Daniel Sullivan are loyal and dedicated city employees with years of service.

In America, there really is no such thing as a "perfect" city, but, unquestionably, one that comes very close, that provides almost every service and amenity that residents and visitors could want, that offers incredible opportunities to businesspeople as well as people of all races, creeds, genders and ages, is the city that is the subject and topic of this book, and in closing it should be made clear—crystal clear—that the city of Hallandale Beach has been, is and will, for many years to come, be Broward County's, if not all of South Florida's, "City of Choice."

Joy Cooper is Hallandale's progressive, forward-looking mayor. *CoHB*.

Vice-mayor (and a great historian in his own right) William A. "Bill" Julian. *CoHB.*

The Hallandale Beach City Commission, *from left*: Commissioners Keith S. London and Dorothy Ross, Mayor Joy Cooper, Vice-mayor Bill Julian and Commissioner Anthony Sanders. *CoHB.*

City Manager D. Mike Good, considered one of the finest municipal managers in Florida. *CoHB.*

Chief of Police Thomas A. Magill is a thirty-six-year employee of the city, having joined the force in 1974. In 2004, he was named chief. *Courtesy HBPD.*

Above: Fire Chief Daniel P. Sullivan, *at left*, with Mayor Joseph Scavo as they accepted the city's new pumper and hose truck on October 24, 2000. *Photo by Sy Lippman, courtesy HBFD.*

Right: Part of the fire department's promotional efforts to bring young people into a career in fire and emergency medical services, this brochure is given to students and young people interested in the department. *Courtesy HBFD.*

This is the chamber's beautiful 1971 promotional for the city as a great place to live, work and do business. It was this booklet that brought Hallandale into the forefront as a place other than the home of Hollywood Kennel Club and Gulfstream Park. *CoHB.*

In 1977, from May 11 until May 21, the city celebrated its fiftieth anniversary. This brochure is the schedule of events. *CoHB.*

It's "a blast from the past" as four of Hallandale's distinguished former mayors pose for a picture in 1993. From left are Samuel B. Waterman, Arthur J. "Sonny" Rosenberg, Aaron I. Canon and Gilbert B. Stein. *Courtesy Arthur Rosenberg.*

Vice-mayor Bill Julian with the archbishop of the Diocese of Miami, John C. Favalora, in October 2009. *Courtesy Vice-mayor Bill Julian.*

Left: Ted Curci stands in front of his family's building. Curcie Industries did much of the land clearing and road building in Hallandale Beach. *CoHB*.

Below: The city's beautiful new government center at 400 South Federal Highway, which opened in 1997. *CoHB*.

Above: A view of the city's famous water tower, looking east from the Intracoastal bridge. *CoHB*.

Right: The sign welcoming visitors to City Beach, managed by Hallandale Parks and Recreation. *CoHB*.

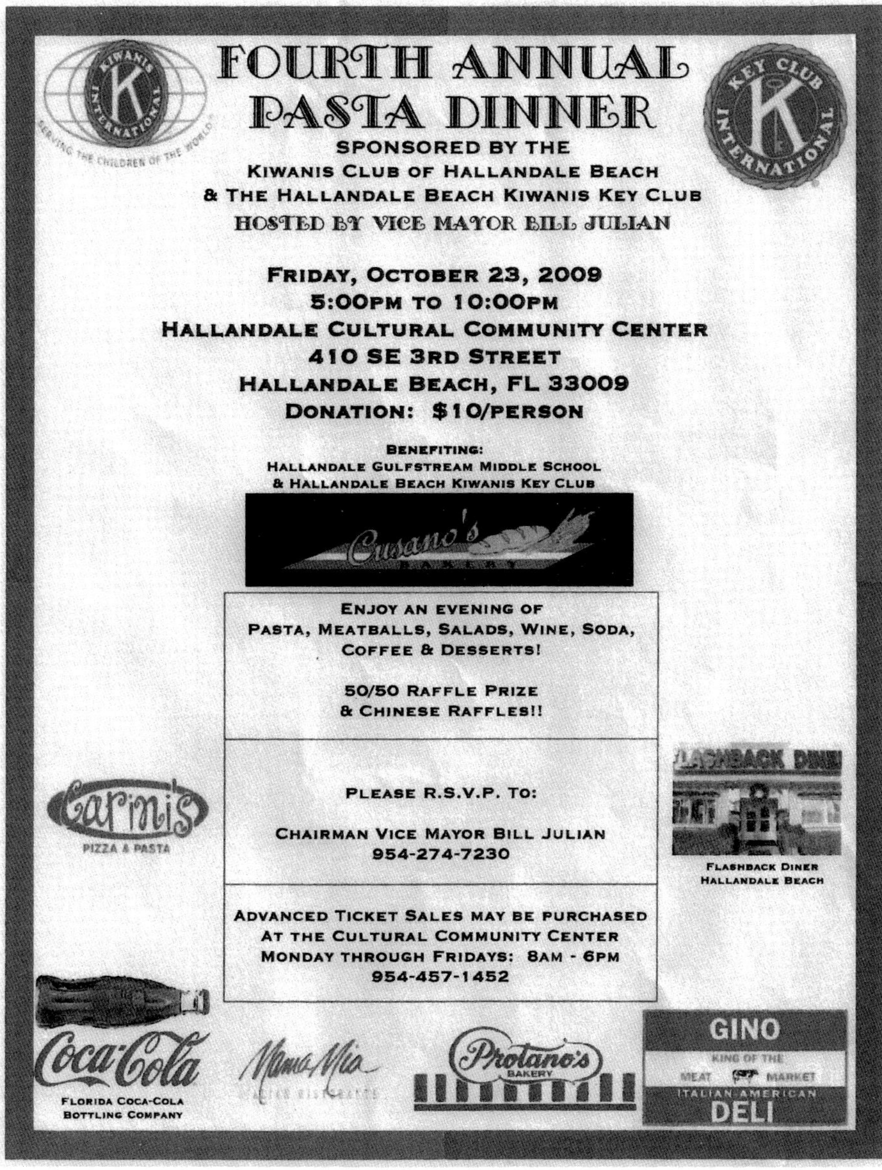

This and next page: Whether the annual Kiwanis Pasta Dinner or the famous Hallandale Symphonic Pops Orchestra, now housed at Gulfstream Village, the city offers something for everyone, every day of the week, in all price ranges and for all tastes in food, entertainment, dining, leisure or community services. Simply put, Hallandale Beach, today, is *the* place to be in South Florida!

HALLANDALE
Symphonic Pops
ORCHESTRA
CONDUCTOR
Peter P. Fuchs
2008 - 2009 SEASON

About the Author

Seth Bramson is South Florida's foremost and leading historian. He is the author of eighteen books on and about South Florida local and Florida transportation history and is the number one published Greater Miami history book author in the country, with fourteen of his eighteen books dealing directly with the villages, towns, cities, counties and people of the Gold Coast.

A graduate of Cornell University's famed School of Hotel Administration, Bramson holds master's degrees from St. Thomas University and Florida International University, both in Miami. In addition to his books, he has authored more than ninety articles, including three in refereed or juried publications. Adjunct professor of history at both Florida International University and Barry University, he is historian-in-residence at Barry as well as at FIU's Osher Lifelong Learning Institute, and in 2008 he was presented with FIU's highest alumni honor, the Torch Award for Community Service.

The founder and current president of the Miami Memorabilia Collectors Club and a founding board member of the Greater North Miami Historical Society, he is a member or board member of almost every historical organization in South Florida.

The senior collector of Florida East Coast Railway, Florida transportation memorabilia, Miami memorabilia and Floridiana in America, his collections of FEC Railway and Florida transportation memorabilia are the largest in the world, while his collections of Miami memorabilia and Floridiana are the largest in private hands in the country.

Company historian of the Florida East Coast Railway, he is one of only two people in the country who bears that official title with an American railroad. He is generally considered the city historian in and for most of the cities he has written about.